MW00484497

1295

La Posta

From the Founding of Mesilla
To Corn Exchange Hotel
To Billy the Kid Museum
To Famous Landmark

First Edition

David G. Thomas

Mesilla Valley History Series, Vol 1

Copyright © 2013 by Doc45 Publishing

All Rights Reserved

This book, or parts thereof, may not be reproduced in any form,
including information storage and retrieval systems,
without explicit permission from Doc45 Publishing,
except for brief quotations included in articles and reviews.

For further information, please address
Doc45 Publishing, P. O. Box 5044, Las Cruces, N. M. 88003
books@doc45.com

To obtain printed or ebooks, visit:
www.doc45.com

Book design and typeset by David Thomas
Cover design by Annika Holmberg and David Thomas

ISBN 978-0-9828709-3-8

Contents

Acknowledgements

I would like to thank Ken McCracken who generously shared his research with me; the Dona Ana County Clerk and employees of the Clerk's Office for supporting and encouraging my efforts to identify early Mesilla property owners; Dan Aranda for sharing his research, translating documents, and finding several egregious errors in the text; Dallas Bash for his work topographically mapping the property blocks discussed in Chapter 2; the archivists at New Mexico State University's Special Collections for their invaluable help in locating documents and photos; Frank H. Parrish for sharing his photographs and information on the Billy the Kid Museum; Joe Lopez for sharing his extensive Mesilla collection; Sally Kading for researching church records; and many others unnamed who aided me in innumerous ways in writing this book.

The inevitable errors are the author's responsibility.

Cover photo courtesy of the Palace of Governors Collection.

Doc45 Publications Web Site

For additional information, visit the web site:

www.doc45.com

Ebook Available

Introduction

This book is about a building, its people, and its place.

The building sits on a lot next to the plaza. The lot is a *"terreno de solar,"* a grant to a Mexican citizen by the state of Chihuahua, Mexico, on which to build a house. By the terms of the grant, the grantee is obliged to own a horse and a gun. Within a year or so the grantee – and his lot – are no longer in Mexico – they are both in the United States. He sells to a merchant, who establishes a store. The merchant takes a partner, and then sells out to his partner. The merchant is Hispanic. The partner is Anglo.

Obviously the story of the building – La Posta -- is inseparable from people and place.[1]

Chapter 1 gives a history of Mesilla as concisely as the author can do it. This is not an A to B to C story. It's more like a puzzle in which only when the pieces are fit into the right place, can you see the picture. Because primary documents are few and hard to find, much false information is in print about Mesilla. The history in this chapter is based on many newly-identified sources and corrects many long-held errors. The 1854 map of the Mesilla Valley by Captain John Pope in this Chapter has never been published previously.

Chapter 2 is an attempt to reconstruct the original owners of the properties around the Mesilla plaza. Think of this as the stories of La Posta's friends and neighbors. This was a laborious, complicated task as the original records are incomplete, in both Spanish and English, and scattered throughout many record books. The early deeds do not always give descriptions of all borders, and the descriptions they do give are of the nature: person X on the north, street on the south, person Y on the east, and person Z on the west. Fortunately, deeds adjacent to the plaza or Main Street usually use that as a border description, so by making paper squares for each deed, the author was able to assemble them so the borders aligned, making it possible to identify where the property was.

You would think that the property records maintained by the county and used to grant titles would identify the full chain of ownership, but they do not. Few go back more than 2 or 3 owners from the current owner.

The reconstruction of the owners around the plaza has produced many rewards, including identifying the location of businesses that were unknown or uncertain before. For example, Chapter 2 identifies the true location of the Overland Mail Offices for the first time. Prior researchers place it in lots B or C, not realizing it occupied two lots and that those lots were D and E (see page 40). Other examples are identifying the locations of the Texas Pacific Hotel and Mesilla Hotel. One final example: prior writers weren't certain where John Lemon lived when he is killed in 1871. His home is identified in Chapter 2.

The maps in Chapter 2 are created using topographic software and lot definitions from the deeds. In virtually all cases, the 140- to 150-year old lot sizes align well with current ownership, showing how persistent over time property definitions are.

The story of the Corn Exchange, a saloon, eating house, and hostelry that in its prime was probably the most famous in New Mexico, is given in Chapter 3. Almost all the major figures of the Lincoln County War stay at the Corn Exchange: John S. Chisum, James Dolan, John Riley, John Kinney, Sheriff William Brady, "Doc" Scurlock, Charles Bowdre, Richard Brewer, Colonel Albert J. Fountain, William Rynerson, Judge Warren Bristol – perhaps even Billy the Kid.

Chapter 4 traces the life of George Griggs, one of the first *"Mesilleros"* and the founder and impresario of the Billy the Kid Museum.

The last chapter recounts the history of La Posta from its beginning with *"three tables and 12 chairs"* to nationally-famous restaurant, and describes the decline and death of George Griggs and the dispersal of his Billy the Kid museum.

A number of major topics play an important role in the history recounted here, but can be covered only in abbreviated form because of space restrictions: the Battle of Mesilla, Civil War, Lincoln County War, and life of Billy the Kid. I have tried to provide enough details on each topic to make its relation to the subject of this book understandable. The reader is directed to other sources for more in-depth information.

Finally, a historiological point. A number of books cite the history of Mesilla as an example of racial conflict between Hispanics and Anglos. It is one of the foundation stones in many of these arguments. There are several accounts of conflict between Hispanics and Anglos in early Mesilla, but almost all on closer examination prove to be examples of what is the real source of conflict in Mesilla: class. Early Anglos and well-off Hispanics got along well and intermarried. Both groups looked down on the poor, which in Mesilla were Hispanics and Indians. Class discrimination was imported from Mexico, where it was a primary factor in social relations. An example of class discrimination is in the awarding of farm grants in Mesilla. No true count of the number of farm grants exists, but based on my research, I believe it was about 78 lots. The Mesilla census of 1851 indicates that there are at least 350 adult males present. Over 250 adult males do not get farm lots. This suggests that Mesilla Civil Colony commissioners Padre Ramon Ortiz and Guadalupe Miranda are using class to determine eligibility. [2]

Racial discrimination did enter into Mesilla life, but it was after the Civil War, and to a large extent it was brought to Mesilla by immigrants from the states that had formed the Confederacy.

Unattributed photos are from the author's collection.

1. *"La Posta"* means stage stop or station.

2. In Doña Ana and Las Cruces, grants were allocated by drawing lots. In Mesilla, the commissioners selected the grantees.

Chapter 1 | Founding of Mesilla

It is not uncommon for the founding of a new town to be straightforward. Known persons show up on a known date and lay out the town. This is not true for *Mesilla,* a Spanish word meaning "small table." The founding of Mesilla is obscured by lack of records, conflicting oral history, Mexican land grants, war, invasion, occupation, peace, threats of war, and border disputes.

Doña Ana Bend Colony Grant

Mexico obtains its independence from Spain in 1821. In the decades that follow, there are numerous efforts by the Mexican government and by individuals to promote the settlement of its northern lands. This is achieved by awarding grants of land to would-be colonists. In the Mesilla Valley, an area roughly defined as stretching from Hatch, New Mexico to the West side of El Paso, Texas, the first land grant by the Mexican government is the Doña Ana Bend Colony Grant.[1] The name of this grant derives from the bend (*"ancon"* in Spanish) in the Rio Grande River about 11 miles north of Mesilla.

In a signed statement dated July 28, 1863, Guadalupe Miranda[2] recalls the origins of the Doña Ana Bend Colony Grant:

> *"On 18 September, 1839, 116 citizens of El Paso[3] addressed a petition, through the Prefect [administrator], to the government of the state of Chihuahua asking to be allowed to settle the lands at the Doña Ana bend. The Prefect of that day – who it was I am not aware – reported favorably, and forwarded the petition. This the Governor and Commanding General took into consideration, and remitting the grant or proposition to the Departmental Assembly which agreed to grant the land to the petitioners, to which decree the Governor, Francisco Garcia Condé[4], decreed, and on 8 July, 1840, he directed that the papers be sent to the Director of the Geographical Board in order that, in accordance with the laws on the subject, he might prescribe the matter in terms in which the division and assignment of the land should be made to the settlers."*

> *"On the 31st of July of the same year the Director remits to the government the grant, accompanied with the regulation formed in accordance with the laws and orders of the Congress of the General Government and of the state, and on the same day the Governor and Commanding General, Francisco Garcia Condé, issued his orders to the Prefect of the town of El Paso to proceed to the granting of said lands, the colony, according to the regulations referred to and orders of the government to be under the immediate supervision of the Prefect of El Paso."*

> *"The circumstance of the war with the savages, and other circumstances not less potent, cause the enterprise to be suspended until the 26th*

of January, 1843, when the persons undertaking to settle went before the Prefect, requesting him to give instructions and orders to the person in charge of the settlers, and these took up their march under the auspices of the peace which have been concluded with the Indians the year before, and 33 only of the settlers having arrived at the place, they on the 2nd of February commenced opening the head of the acequia, although working several days; but, owing to some circumstance or another, they begin slowly to retire, until about 14 settlers were left, who in that year planted on a small-scale the same yielding according to the work they had done, which aroused the ambition of the petitioners who had left, as well as many others who until then, had not calculated upon such an enterprise." [5]

"Acequia" is Spanish for "irrigation ditch." To feed themselves in this dry environment, the colonists needed to irrigate the lands they wanted to cultivate. This is accomplished by digging a main irrigation ditch, an *"acequia madre"* (mother ditch), from the Rio Grande River, and then digging branch ditches to farming plots. The critical first task of the new Doña Ana settlement is to dig an acequia madre, which is begun February 2, 1843, Saint Candelaria's day.[6]

As Miranda noted, digging the acequia madre for the new colony is an immense job, and all but 14 settlers abandon it. To achieve the necessary gravity flow, the ditch had to come out of the river about 2-3 miles above the colony. The colonists had only wooden spades and hoes to dig with. That first year, the colonists managed to cultivate only one small block of land.[7]

The importance of the day the acequia madre was begun is recognized by the colonists by naming their church Nuestra Señora de la Candelaria de Doña Ana.

On January 19, 1844, Colonel Mauricio Ugarte, Military Commander of the Frontier, travels from El Paso del Norte to Doña Ana to allocate farm lots to the colonists. The original 14 are given the privilege of selecting the lot they want. Other colonists who are accompanying Ugarte draw for their lots. Heads of households are allocated lots that are 780 ½ varas on a side, non-heads of households are allocated lots that are 780 ½ varas in length and 390 ¼ varas in width. 47 of the larger lots are allocated and 22 of the smaller ones.[8] A census taken that day shows the colony consists of 107 men, 59 women, and 95 children.[9]

The *"vara"* was a standard unit of measurement in Spain and her New World conquests, but the vara did not have one fixed length. There were several different varas that varied slightly in length, but the one that was used in Doña Ana and later in Mesilla is 1 vara = 32.9927 inches.[10]

Although Colonel Ugarte allocates lots on his visit to Doña Ana, he fails to provide written titles. This is accomplished by Miranda:

"On the 22nd of January, 1845, I, being the Prefect of El Paso, and as one of the colonists… determined to forward the documents, together with the respective plats I had formed, and to authorize the principal Justice of Doña Ana to measure off and distribute the lands and issue the titles to the parties interested respectively, which up to that time had not been issued them…. Mr. Pablo Melendrez [then] did so…." [11]

Mexican-American War

Doña Ana is still struggling to establish itself when the United States declares war on Mexico on May 13, 1846. The origins of the Mexican-American war are in border disputes between Texas and Mexico, not settled by the Texas War of Independence – disputes picked up and continued by the United States after Texas becomes a state.

During the Mexican-American war, the United States attacks Mexico on numerous fronts: from Texas into Mexico, into California by land and sea, through the Mexican port of Veracruz, and into New Mexico by way of the Santa Fe Trail.[12]

The New Mexico offensive is led by General Stephen Watts Kearny. Kearny's army of about 1,700 men, consisting of one Dragoon company, one volunteer infantry regiment, and one artillery company, leaves Fort Leavenworth in late June, 1846. On August 18, 1846, Kearny's men successfully occupy Santa Fe, New Mexico, without a fight.[13]

After spending several months battling Indians, not Mexicans, Kearny with about 100 Dragoons departs for California to aid the United States forces there. About the same time, Colonel Alexander W. Doniphan leads 850 mounted riflemen south following the Rio Grande River with the goal of reaching El Paso del Norte and then Chihuahua.[14]

On December 22, 1846, Doniphan and his men *"fatigued with marching, faint with hunger, and benumbed by the piercing winds"* reach Doña Ana, where they are received without animosity and sold food and animal feed. *"Here they feasted and reposed."* After several days, the force leaves that welcome place and on December 24th reaches a site about 26 miles south of Doña Ana known as Brazito, where they make camp. It being Christmas Eve, they celebrate by singing songs and firing their guns.[15]

Breaking camp the next morning, Doniphan's men continue toward El Paso del Norte. Scouts had been warning Doniphan for several days that a Mexican force was in the area, but he is still surprised to be confronted by a Mexican battalion of about 1,200 men under General Antonio Ponce de Leon. In the ensuing 40-minute battle, the Mexicans are defeated, with 71 killed and 150 wounded. Eight of Doniphan's men are wounded, with none killed. This easy victory is considered a Christmas present by the Americans, made more so by finding *"sacks and wallets of provisions, and gourds of the delicious wines of El Paso"* left behind by the fleeing Mexicans.[16]

Following the Battle of Brazito, Doniphan occupies El Paso del Norte, and after a few weeks preparation, continues on to Chihuahua, which he occupies after defeating the city's defenders in the Battle of Sacramento on February 28, 1847.[17]

The attack on Mexico through multiple fronts finally produces victory for the United States on February 2, 1848, when the Treaty of Guadalupe Hidalgo is signed. The treaty concedes Mexico's vast territories of New Mexico and northern California, territories which include land now defined as the states of New Mexico, Arizona, Utah, Nevada, California, and parts of Colorado, Kansas, and Oklahoma. In exchange the United States agrees to pay Mexico $15 million and to pay damage claims of Americans against Mexico up to $3.2 million.[18]

Mexico agrees, after strenuous negotiations, on a border between the two countries that defines the Rio Grande River as the Texas border to the southern edge of New Mexico, thence west along the line that Mexico traditionally recognized as being the southern border of the Mexican territory of New Mexico to the Gila River, then along the Gila River to where it joins the Colorado River, and then, as the last leg, a straight line to about one mile below San Diego Bay on the Pacific Ocean.[19] Attached to the treaty is a map published by J. Disturnell in 1847 containing unrecognized inaccuracies, the worst being the placing of El Paso del Norte 15 minutes north of the 32nd parallel instead of 15 minutes south of the parallel, where it actually is.[20]

This boundary definition is less exact than the signers believe, and will lead to further serious boundary problems between Mexico and the United States.

The treaty is ratified by the U. S. Senate on March 10, 1848, and proclaimed on July 4, 1848.[21]

With the acquisition of New Mexico, the United States sets about organizing it as an American territory. Besides establishing an appointed government, the United States sends troops to occupy the land and protect the occupants from Indians. On November 7, 1848, Company H, First Dragoons, consisting of 87 men and commanded by Lieutenant Delos B. Sackett is stationed in Doña Ana.[22] Several of the men in this company will remain in the Mesilla Valley and become prominent citizens after being discharged in 1851.[23]

Las Cruces

1849 is a brutal year for Indian attacks on settlers at Doña Ana. The relative peace that had existed between the settlers and native-Americans when the town was founded is destroyed by the Mexican-American War. The war interrupts Mexico's policies of *"pacification"* by providing food and goods to Indians, and also offers the Indians a lucrative opportunity to gain by raiding, taking cattle, horses, sheep, and even captives.

Here's an account of a raid on Doña Ana by Captain Enoch Steen, who succeeds Lt. Sackett as military commander at Doña Ana:

> *"On Saturday, the 2nd instant about 8 o'clock a report was brought to my quarters that the Apaches had made a descent upon the herds grazing in the rear of the town & driven off the stock after wounding four Mexican herders, one of whom is since dead, & carrying away one boy."* [24]

Indian raiding is so bad that *"farms could not be tilled and had the [American] government not issued them [the settlers at Doña Ana] flour and provisions, there would have been much suffering."* [25]

The tolls of Indian raiding, overcrowding, and lack of opportunity generate a desire in many Doña Ana residents to create a new town. In December, 1848, a group of settlers establishes a camp at the present site of Las Cruces. They began digging an acequia madre to the Rio Grande on January 3, 1849. In response to their request, Pablo Melendrez[26], *"alcalde"* (mayor/justice of the peace) of Doña Ana, asks Lieutenant Sackett to survey and layout the new townsite.[27]

Lieutenant Sackett agrees. When Sackett with five soldiers to help him arrives at the Las Cruces camp site, he finds it has grown to 120 people with many living in brush huts. Sackett lays out *"three streets running north and south – Church, Main and Water streets – together with the east and west streets intersecting."* A drawing is held to allocate lots to heads of families who are present.[28]

As with Doña Ana, the Catholic Church in Las Cruces is named for the saint's day on which the acequia madre is begun, La Iglesia de Saint Genevieve.

Bartlett-Condé Survey

The Treaty of Guadalupe Hidalgo specifies that the border between Mexico and the United States will be established by a survey to be carried out by a joint commission. In recognition of this treaty requirement, Mexico appoints General Pedro García Condé [29], an experienced engineer and surveyor, to lead its side. The United States appoints John Russell Bartlett[30] its commissioner. Bartlett was not a surveyor or an engineer, which is not considered a disqualification because he has surveyors and engineers on his staff. But Bartlett proves to be fundamentally ill-suited for his assignment, and partisan politics and conflict between the military and civilian members will cause huge problems within his commission.

The commission decides to begin at the Pacific Ocean, and on October 10, 1849, it marks its first point there. Encountering great difficulties, the commission completes most of its survey across California by February 15, 1850, when it decides to suspend that portion of the survey and resume at the eastern border at El Paso del Norte. During this period of the commission's operation, Bartlett has not yet been appointed to head the American side.[31]

Bartlett is appointed on June 19, 1850, and on December 3, 1850, the joint commission meets in El Paso del Norte to begin its work.[32]

The Treaty of Guadalupe Hidalgo specifies that the border beginning where Texas and New Mexico meet and running west will follow the traditional border between New Mexico and the State of Chihuahua to the Gila River. But because the Disturnell Map attached to the treaty has misplaced El Paso del Norte by 30 minutes, the two commissioners have to negotiate the location of the starting point. Condé argues that the starting point should be 32 degrees, 22 minutes north latitude, which Bartlett eventually accepts on December 25, 1850, even though the official surveyor on Bartlett's team strenuously disputes the point.[33]

The 32° 22′ starting point is a Christmas present for Mexico, because it places the United States border about 30 miles further north than the traditionally accepted border of New Mexico. Condé writes his superiors:

> *"The most vital question… is resolved favorably in the interests of the Nation. The boundary is not finally that which Disturnell traced…. It is the parallel of 32° 22′ of latitude, nearly thirty-seven geographic miles straight north from the town [El Paso del Norte], embracing the dam, woods, and the population of Mesilla…." [34]*

The border commission continues its work over the next seven years, interrupted by political disputes between the two countries, geological obstacles and temperature extremes, huge delays, internal conflict, funding problems, surveying complications, conflict with Native Americans, the appointment of a new American commissioner, and the signing of the Gadsden Purchase. The final meeting of the commission is September 30, 1857.[35]

La Mesilla

Before Mesilla is a settlement, it almost certainly is a *"paraje,"* a camp along the trail from Chihuahua to Santa Fe.[36] This suggests attractive features to the location: closeness to the river for water, Cottonwood trees for shelter and fuel, and the small mesa from which the name comes, which provides good views of the river valley. There may have been attempts to live, not just camp, at the site when the Indian threat was not too great. It would be a marginal existence without acequias to irrigate crop land.

Following the conclusion of the Mexican-American War there is a population explosion in the Mesilla Valley. The large majority of these are Mexicans, immigrants from El Paso del Norte and Chihuahua and farmers and laborers being pushed off border lands in Texas that had been previously considered part of Mexico. There is also an influx of merchants, adventurers, and soldiers from northern New Mexico and the United States.

The population growth that led to the creation of Las Cruces in January, 1849, probably leads to settlers also gathering at the Mesilla site, which was across the Rio Grande River from Las Cruces. A letter forwarded to the Governor of Chihuahua on August 15, 1849, from an official in El Paso del Norte states:

> *"I enclose for Your Excellency a petition from three individuals of Senecú village and in the name of 15 more have placed before this judgeship asking that the site of La [line through] Mecia be pointed out to them in order that they may move their people, and that they may know under what country's law they must make their petition."*[37]

The tone of this letter suggests that the petitioners consider the Mesilla site to be more than a spot in the wilderness.

The only clearly documented account of the first settlers of Mesilla is that given by Bartlett in his published account of the Bartlett-Condé commission:

> *"On the 1st of March, 1850, sixty Mexicans, with Don Rafael Ruelas[38] as their head, most of whom had been domiciled at Doña Ana, abandoned their homes on account of their many grievances, and moved to the lands known as the Mesilla, where they established themselves."* [39]

In March of 1850, both Mexico and the United States assume that Mesilla is part of the new United States territory of New Mexico, since it had always been part of New Mexico. This changes when Bartlett and Condé sign formal papers recognizing the 32° 22′ boundary on April 24, 1851, and began surveying.[40]

Both Mexicans and Americans in the area now believe that Mesilla is again part of Mexico.

Thomas J. Bull[41], in testimony given in Federal Court when the legal status of Mesilla is being determined by the United States Court of Private Land Claims, says that he came to the Doña Ana area in 1849. He had accompanied Doniphan on his march to Chihuahua as an un-enlisted clerk, passing through Doña Ana when Doniphan did and returning shortly after the end of the Mexican-American War. He says that he moved to Mesilla in March or April of 1851 when it was still considered part of the United States. He also says that the townsite was surveyed at that time and divided into 160-acre lots, measuring 960 by 960 varas.[42]

Bull testifies further that as soon as he learned that Mesilla was part of Mexico, he moved to Las Cruces, because he wanted to be in the United States.[43]

The Mesilla acequia madre is begun March 1, 1851, San Albino's day, giving Mesilla's Catholic Church its name: La Iglesia de San Albino.[44]

Moving fast to capitalize on the 32° 22′ boundary, the government of Chihuahua passes the Colonization Act of May 22, 1851. The Act permits the establishment of settlements at places *"considered most appropriate"* and authorizes the appointment of a commissioner to oversee the settlements, who has the power to define common lands, set aside land for a church and plaza, issue legal titles to lands, specify the boundaries of the settlement, and establish a government.[45]

Two days later, on May 24, Padre Ramon Ortiz[46] is appointed Commissioner General of Immigration for the state of Chihuahua. Ortiz is the curate (assistant priest) of the Catholic Church in El Paso del Norte. A strong Mexican nationalist, he was one of the men who had encouraged General Ponce de Leon to fight at the Battle of Brazito.[47]

By August, 1851, Ortiz is in Mesilla where he begins to issue land grants to settlers. The first Mesilla deed recorded in the Doña Ana County Courthouse is to Antonio Uribes on August 8 for a farm lot. The deed is signed by Ortiz as commissioner and cites the Act of May 22 as the authority for the deed. The deed mandates that the grantee be armed and own a horse so he can defend the colony if needed. It also mandates that within three months he plant the borders of his lot with fruit trees or other trees useful to the colonists, and that within two years he grow a crop. He is forbidden during the first four years of ownership from renting, mortgaging, or selling his land.[48]

On August 13, Ortiz issues additional farm grants, including one to Rafael Ruelas, the settlement leader.[49] On August 16, he issues more, and continues to do so into 1852. All grants have the same restrictions.

Under the Mexican colonization laws, there were two kinds of settler land grants: *"terreno de riego"* and *"terreno de solar."* The first means irrigated (farm) land, the second house land.

The first land grants recorded in the deed books are terreno de riegos, like the one issued to Antonio Uribes. The deed records for this time period are incomplete with missing pages. Oritz issues documents to the grantees and when that person sells their land, the owner's copy of the grant is entered into the county deed books – so these records are scattered throughout the books. Uribes' farm grant is recorded in deed book "B" on March 29, 1856.[50]

As Bull testifies, Mesilla was surveyed into 160-acre lots when it was considered U. S. territory. He further states:

"Ortiz found that if he gave [160] acres of land to each one that he would not have enough to go around..., [so] he divided these... lots into three pieces, which would be [53 1/3] acres in each piece. There were a great many people there, and then some more people began to come in there to get more land, and he had to cut down the allotments; some to about one hundred and twenty varas."

"All these allotments were generally... nine hundred and sixty varas long. One hundred and fifty-three acres of land [was] nine hundred and sixty varas long and three hundred and twenty varas wide." [51]

Samuel "Sam" Gore Bean[52], in the same court case, testifies:

"I came to Doña Ana county in 1849.... When the grant was first settled the settlers built temporary houses.... Afterwards they built permanent houses...." [53]

In late 1851, the state of Chihuahua authorizes a formal census of Mesilla. The result is a count of 1,230 people, most of whom list their occupation as laborer. All names enumerated are Hispanic.[54]

With Mesilla well established, Ortiz needs to legalize it. On January 20, 1852, Ortiz issues the Mesilla Civil Colony Grant. The grant states that the colony has met the legal requirements of being established, developed, and divided into parcel and house lots; has been issued common lands; and contains more than a thousand people.[55]

In Washington, D. C, the government of the United States had initially been willing to accept the 32° 22′ border point agreed to by Bartlett. This opinion changes when it becomes apparent that the resulting boundary does not agree with the Disturnell map or with the traditional border of New Mexico. Newspaper editorials begin to refer to Bartlett's decision as *"an enormous blunder,"* giving away a 34 x 175 mile area, about 6,000 square miles.[56]

On December 20, 1852, the U. S. Congress officially repudiates the 32° 22′ border point – and by dissolving and reconstituting the border commission, fires Bartlett as commissioner.[57] He is replaced by William H. Emory, the surveyor who objected to Barlett's selection of the 32° 22′ border point.[58]

Prior to the repudiation of the 32° 22′ boundary, there is some talk on the American side of going to war over the disputed area. After the repudiation, this becomes the dominant public opinion, with few dissenting voices. Naturally Mexico responds by stating She is fully willing to go to war to protect what is Hers, granted legally by the signed agreement between Bartlett and Condé.

This war tension flashes white hot on March 13, 1853, when William Carr Lane, the Governor of the Territory of New Mexico, issues a proclamation claiming United States' jurisdiction over Mesilla. After reciting the arguments for U. S. ownership, the proclamation states:

"I, William Carr Lane... upon my own official responsibility and without orders from the cabinet at Washington, do hereby, in behalf of the

United States, retake possession of the said disputed territory... until the question of boundary shall be determined...." [59]

Lane issues the statement at Doña Ana, where he is visiting, staying at the house of Pablo Melendrez.[60]

Mexico responds by withdrawing its minister from Washington and ordering troops to Mesilla. On April 7, 1853, Angel Trias, the Governor of Chihuahua, leaves Chihuahua with 750 men and 150 officers. He arrives at El Paso del Norte on April 25 and occupies Mesilla a day or two later.[61]

In the midst of this military response, the Mexican government fails, permitting Antonio Lopez de Santa Ana to take power, which he does formally on April 30, 1853. This is Santa Ana's eleventh (and last) term as President of Mexico. Santa Ana was president when Texas obtained its independence from Mexico, he was president when the Treaty of Guadalupe Hidalgo was signed, and he is president during this crisis.[62]

Because Padre Ortiz is an opponent of Santa Ana and his supporters, he is removed as Commissioner of Immigration on March 23, 1853, and replaced by Guadalupe Miranda,[63] Mexican consul at Franklin.[64]

On July 30, 1853, Governor Trias orders his troops out of Mesilla and back to Chihuahua. Clearly in a friendly mood, he and a number of his officers stop at Fort Fillmore, in United States territory, for several days, where they are welcomed and entertained. His occupation of Mesilla has lasted just over a month.[65]

August 3 and 4, 1853, are busy days for new Immigration Commissioner Miranda. On August 3 he splits off a southern chunk of the Mesilla Civil Colony Grant into a separate Santo Tomas de Yturbide Colony Grant and issues legal titles for both grants. On August 4, he surveys the borders of the grants and places landmarks, declaring:

> *"...common lands, water, game, fisheries, stone, fruit trees and things the [common] land produces to be for the common benefit of the residents of the Mesilla Colony."* [66]

Miranda also forbids Mesilla residents from shopping in the United States:

> *"I am informed that two wagon loads of people from Mesilla, a few days ago, went to Las Cruces to get salt, and since this is a territory of the United States you are hereby ordered that this will not be repeated."* [67]

In November, 1853, an interesting clash occurs between Mesilla and Las Cruces. On January 1 of that year, Las Cruces is appointed the county seat.[68] The District Court meets for the first time in Las Cruces in November and Pedro Jose Borule, a resident of Mesilla, is indicted for killing the Mescalero Indian Chief Cuentas Azules.[69] The judge orders the arrest of Borule. The marshal and a posse travel to Mesilla where they learn that Borule is within the settlement, but Rafael Ruelas, as alcalde, refuses to accept American jurisdiction. The Americans back down, realizing that it would take military force to overcome the settlers' resistance.[70]

Gadsden Purchase

In early August, 1853, a new U. S. Minister to Mexico, James Gadsden, arrives in Mexico City. Gadsden, an ex-Army officer, had been president of the Southern Carolina Railroad Company from 1840 to 1850. He is a long-term and untiring advocate of building a transcontinental railroad across the United States, and he favors a southern route through New Mexico. He and other advocates of the southern route are worried that Bartlett's 32° 22′ agreement has made a southern route impossible.[71]

In Mexico, Gadsden finds Santa Ana's government in political and financial turmoil. Santa Ana is worried that a second war will break out with the United States over the 32° 22′ disputed section, and that in a second war, Mexico will lose even more territory.[72] In the United States, newspaper editors are warning: *"There is no longer room for doubt that we are on the verge of a fresh conflict with Mexico."* [73]

Taking advantage of Santa Ana's financial situation and the fears of war, Gadsden is able to negotiate the purchase of a 38,000-square-mile block of land that includes the 32° 22′ disputed section and stretches to Yuma, Arizona. The purchase agreement is signed secretly by the Mexican government and Gadsden on December 30, 1853. Both sides agree to keep the agreement secret until approved by the U. S. Congress. The agreement provides for the United States to pay $15 million dollars for the land and to pay claims against the Mexican government by American citizens up to $5 million.[74]

The U. S. Congress rejects the treaty on April 17, 1854. But in a second vote on April 25, 1854, Congress approves the treaty, with the changes that the land area is reduced by 9,000 square miles and the price consequently is reduced to $10 million. No money is authorized for claims against Mexico.[75]

The Gadsden Purchase, referred to in Mexico as *"El Tratado de Mesilla,"* is proclaimed on June 10, 1854.[76] $7 million is paid that day to Mexico. By the time the last $3 million is paid, Santa Ana has been deposed.[77]

On September 25, 1854, Domingo Cubero[78] of Mesilla writes to Lt. Col. Dixon S. Miles of Fort Fillmore acknowledging that Mesilla will shortly be under United States jurisdiction and asking for military help in protecting the town from Indian depredations.[79]

The United States takes official possession of Mesilla on November 16, 1854, in a public ceremony on the plaza.[80] Dr. James A. Bennett describes the event as follows:

> *"This morning the parade started with General Garland and Governor Meriwether[81] leading it, followed by our Company, two companies of Infantry, Company B, 1st Dragoons, and the 3rd Infantry Band. We crossed the river and took possession of the town and valley of Mesilla in the name of the United States Government. A speech was made by the Governor and translated into Spanish. A flag staff was raised. The "Stars and Stripes" were then floated from the top and three times three loud cheers were given. The Band played: Hail Columbia, Yankee Doodle, and the Star Spangled Banner. The Mexicans, holding office, swore allegiance to our government.*

All Mexicans such as did not wish to obey our laws were notified to leave and to take refuge in Mexican dominions. " [82]

The transfer of power between the two countries was memorialized years later by Albert Fountain, Jr. Drawing upon first hand accounts available to him at the time, Fountain painted the settlers of Mesilla lining the plaza and watching the ceremony, with rows of troops standing at attention.

In Mexico, the annexation of Mesilla by the United States is not well received. Because the final $3 million had not yet been paid, the Mexican government denounces the action as presumptuous and unjustified.[83]

With Mesilla again an American town, what was it like? It is still a primitive frontier settlement and a dangerous place to live. In a letter to General Garland, 2nd Lt. Laurens O'Bannon, after visiting Mesilla, describes it as *"but jacal building of the most indifferent kind, very small, too much so for comfort."* [84] Dr. Bennett, in contrast, describes it as *"a pretty town which is filled with very pretty women."* [85]

1855 is a turning point for Mesilla. Becoming part of the United States opens it up to a wave of immigration and development that rapidly leads it to becoming the largest town between Galveston and San Francisco.

Timeline

- August 24, 1821 – Mexican Independence
- September 18, 1839 – Doña Ana Bend Colony petition
- July 8, 1840 – Doña Ana Bend Colony petition granted
- February 2, 1843 – First Doña Ana settlers arrive and begin digging acequia madre
- January 19, 1844 – Farm lots allocated at Doña Ana
- May 13, 1846 – United States declares war on Mexico
- August 18, 1846 – General Kearny occupies Santa Fe
- December 22, 1846 – Colonel Doniphan occupies Doña Ana
- December 25, 1846 – Battle of Brazito
- February 28, 1847 – Battle of Sacramento
- February 2, 1848 – Treaty of Guadalupe Hidalgo signed
- March 10, 1848 – U. S. ratifies Treaty of Guadalupe Hidalgo
- July 4, 1848 – Treaty of Guadalupe Hidalgo proclaimed
- November 7, 1848 – U. S. Dragoons arrive at Doña Ana
- December, 1848 – Settlers gather at Las Cruces site
- January 3, 1849 – Lt. Sackett lays out Las Cruces townsite
- January 3, 1849 – Settlers start digging the Las Cruces acequia madre
- October 10, 1849 – Border Commission marks first border point
- March 1, 1850 – Rafael Ruelas leads 60 settlers to Mesilla site
- June 19, 1850 – Bartlett appointed U. S. Border Commissioner
- December 3, 1850 – Border Commission begins survey at El Paso del Norte
- December 25, 1850 – Bartlett accepts mistaken 32° 22′ border point
- March 1, 1851 – Mesilla acequia madre begun
- March/April, 1851 – Bull moves to Mesilla
- April 24, 1851 – Bartlett and Condé sign formal papers accepting the 32° 22′ point

- May 22, 1851 – State of Chihuahua passes Colonization Act
- May 24, 1851 – Padre Ortiz appointed Immigration Commissioner
- August 8, 1851 – Ortiz issues first Mesilla deed to Antonio Uribes
- Late 1851 – Census of Mesilla counts 1230 people
- December 19, 1851 – Commissioner Condé dies.
- January 20, 1852 – Ortiz issues Mesilla Civil Colony Grant
- December 20, 1852 – U. S. Congress repudiates 32° 22′ border point
- March 13, 1853 – Governor Lane claims U. S. ownership of Mesilla
- April 1, 1853 – Guadalupe Miranda replaces Ortiz
- April 25, 1853 – Governor Trias arrives in El Paso del Norte with troops
- April 26-27, 1853 – Governor Trias occupies Mesilla
- April 30, 1853 – Santa Ana takes power as president of Mexico
- July 30, 1853 – Governor Trias leaves Mesilla
- August 3, 1853 – Miranda creates Santo Tomas de Yturbide Colony Grant
- August 4, 1853 – Miranda issues legal titles to Mesilla and Yturbide Grants
- Early August – James Gadsden arrives in Mexico City as U. S. Minister
- November, 1853 – Americans attempt to make an arrest in Mesilla
- December 30, 1853 – Gadsden Purchase signed secretly in Mexico
- April 17, 1854 – Gadsden Purchase rejected by U. S. Congress
- April 25, 1854 – Gadsden Purchase ratified by U. S. Congress
- June 10, 1854 – Gadsden Purchase proclaimed and $7 million paid Mexico
- November 16, 1854 – U. S. takes possession of Mesilla.
- September 30, 1857 – Last official meeting of the Border Commission

Photos

Nuestra Señora de la Candelaria de Doña Ana. Restored in 1991-94. The exact date of the building of the church is unknown. Core samples taken from the church's vigas (rafters) date to the early 1860s.

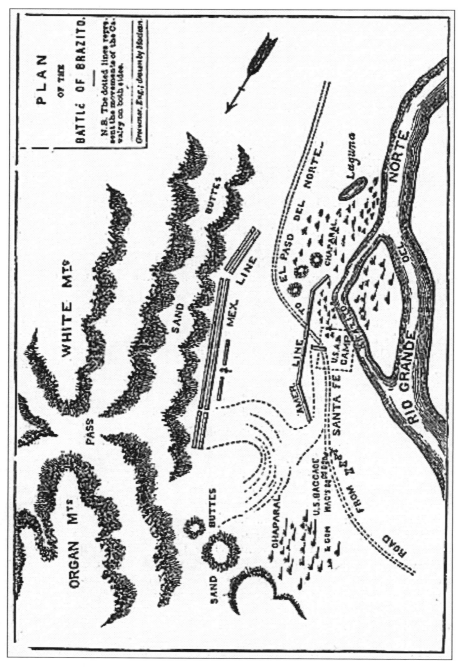

"Brazito" is Spanish for "little arm," which refers to the split in the river. Map from ***Doniphan's Expedition*** by John T. Hughes.

Catholic Church.

LAS CRUCES, NEW MEXICO,

2709

La Iglesia de Saint Genevieve, about 1886. The church was torn down in the 1970s.

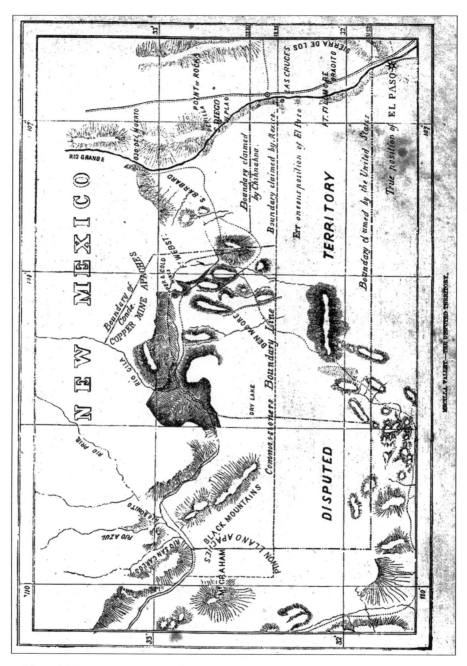

Map of Disputed Territory, Bartlett's *"Enormous Blunder," Illustrated News*, June 4, 1853. Note correct and erroneous El Paso del Norte locations.

Monument commemorating Point No. 1 of the 32° 22´ boundary line agreed to by Bartlett and Condé. The monument is located about half a mile north of the old town of Picacho.

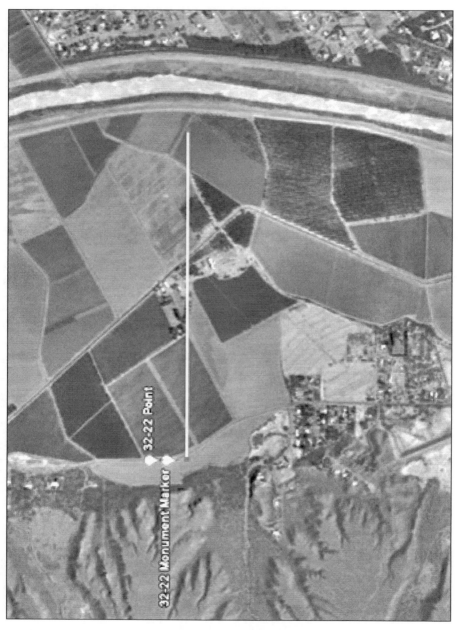

Satellite image showing location of the Commemorative Monument, the true 32° 22´ point, and the distance to the Rio Grande River. The original Bartlett-Condé marker was about 100 feet west of the river. No trace of the original Bartlett-Condé marker remains.

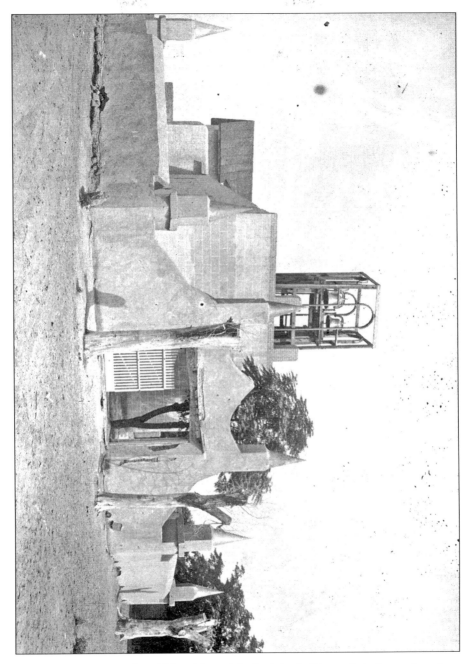

First La Iglesia de San Albino. The original adobe bell tower is being replaced with a brick tower. About 1885. Courtesy Palace of Governors.

La Iglesia de San Albino about 1887. Courtesy Joe Lopez.

The new La Iglesia de San Albino, 1908. Courtesy Joe Lopez.

Corner stone of San Albino. Father Grange, who paid $8,500 of the $15,000 that the new church cost, accused the builder, Joseph H. Stahl, of inflating the cost. In retaliation, Father Grange scraped the builder's name from the corner stone.

San Albino today. Designated a Basilica on November 1, 2008.

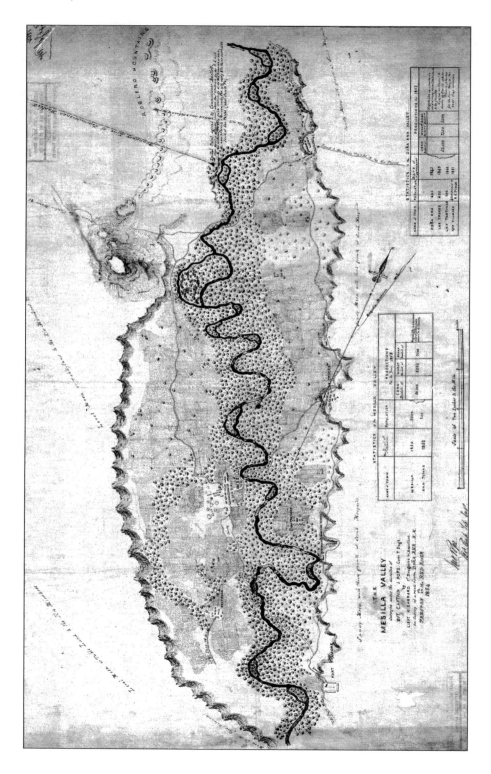

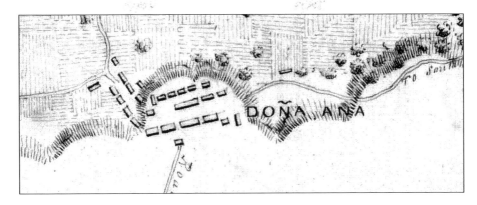

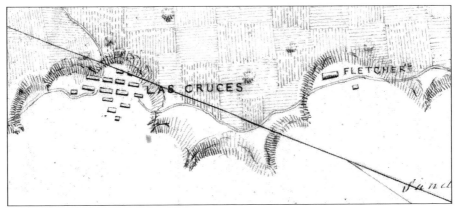

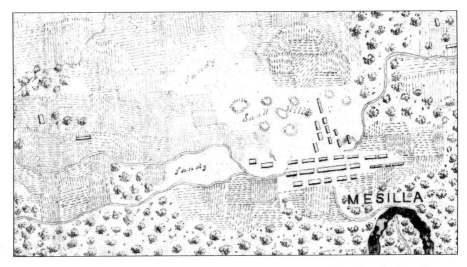

Left: 1854 Map of Mesilla Valley by Captain John Pope. Top: Details from the map showing Dona Ana, Las Cruces, and Mesilla. NARA, RG 77.

Mouth of the acequia madre that provides irrigation water to Mesilla and Las
Cruces. On this date, January 5, 2012, the Rio Grande is completely dry.

Footnotes

1. Two prior Mesilla Valley grants had been issued by Spain: the Santa Teresa Grant in 1790 and the Bracito (Brazito) Grant in 1805. There is no sign that the first one led to any settlement. The Brazito Grant is occupied for several years in 1824 or 1825 but abandoned because of Indian depredations. J. J. Bowden, *Spanish and Mexican Land Grants in the Chihuahuan Acquisition* (Texas Western Press, University of Texas at El Paso, 1971).

2. Born December 13, 1800, at El Paso del Norte, into a wealthy family. After receiving an excellent education in Chihuahua, Miranda moves to Santa Fe and establishes a school. In 1839, he is appointed Secretary of New Mexico. During this time he is one of the recipients of what is later called the Maxwell Land Grant. By 1845, he is prefect (administrator) of El Paso del Norte and in that office becomes one of the settlers of Doña Ana. In 1851, he obtains a grant for land north of El Paso (Texas), a grant never recognized by the U. S. In 1853, he is appointed consul for Mexico at El Paso (Texas). In April of that year he is appointed Immigration Commissioner for New Mexico and moves to Mesilla. In 1868, Miranda sells his interest in the Maxwell Grant for $2,745. He dies February 26, 1888, in Chihuahua.

3. El Paso in this document refers to El Paso del Norte, present day Juarez, Mexico. The settlement on the Texas side of the border is called Franklin at this time.

4. Brother of Pedro Garcia Condé. See note 29.

5. Signed statement of Guadalupe Miranda provided to the Surveyor General of New Mexico, Town of Doña Ana, July 28, 1863. Records of the Bureau of Land Management.

6. *Rio Grande Republican*, January 6, 1899.

7. Bowden, *Spanish and Mexican Land Grants in the Chihuahuan Acquisition*, p 69.

8. Signed statement of Guadalupe Miranda, July 28, 1863.

9. *Executive Documents of the Senate of the United States*, Vol. 1581, 1873-74. Doc. No. 43, p 81.

10. Lionel Cajen Fritze, *History of La Mesilla and Her Mesilleros* (Book Publishers of El Paso, 1995), p 25.

11. Signed statement of Guadalupe Miranda, July 28, 1863.

12. John S. D. Eisenhower, *So Far From God* (University of Oklahoma Press, 1989).

13. Eisenhower, *So Far From God*, p 209.

14. Eisenhower, *So Far From God,* p 234.

15. John T. Hughes, *Doniphan's Expedition* (Published by U. P. James, Cincinnati, 1847), p 95.

16. Hughes, *Doniphan's Expedition,* p 97.

17. Eisenhower, *So Far From God,* p 244.

18. Eisenhower, *So Far From God*, p 363.

19. Joseph Richard Werne, *The Imaginary Line* (Texas Christian University Press, 2007), p 11.

20. Werne, *The Imaginary Line*, p 55.

21. Robert M. Utley, *Changing Course* (Southwest Parks and Monuments Association, 1996), p 14.

22. *Rio Grande Republican*, April 14, 1885.

23. Louis W. Geck, Charles H. Coleman, Conrad Aubel, Adolphe Lea, Co. H 1st Dragoons; Herman Greenwald, Co. I 1st Dragoons; Christian Duper and George A. Ackenback, Co. D and Co. A 2nd Dragoons -- all life-long area residents who came to Doña Ana in 1848-49. See note 70, Chapter 2.

24. Richard Wadsworth, *"The Last Dragoon: Enoch Steen at Doña Ana,"* Southern New Mexico Historical Review, Vol. VII, No. 1, p 1.

25. *Rio Grande Republican*, April 14, 1885.

26. Born 1787. Melendrez is appointed alcalde of Doña Ana on January 26, 1844; is the first elected Probate Judge of Doña Ana County; is elected to the New Mexico Territorial Legislature in 1867; dies in Mesilla on June 16, 1868.

27. *Rio Grande Republican*, January 6, 1899.

28. *Rio Grande Republican*, April 14, 1885.

29. Born February 6, 1806. After training as a military cadet, Pedro Condé attends Mexico's premier engineering academy, Colegio de Minería. By the time he joins Bartlett as a Border Commissioner, he has vast experience as a military leader, educator, political leader, and surveyor. He dies December 19, 1851, at Arizpe, Sonora, from illness directly attributable to the terrible hardship endured by the surveyors. *"It was a singular coincidence that the General, who had left Arispe when quite young, had not visited it again until he was taken there to die; and that this event should occur in the very house in which he drew his first breath."* -- Barlett

30. Born October 23, 1805. Trained as an accountant, with skills as an artist and a draftsman, Bartlett had spent 15 years running a bookstore in New York City and writing books when he is appointed U. S. Commissioner to the Border Commission. His appointment is the product of political influence. Because the Commission's mandate includes gathering biological, ethnographic, and geological data while surveying, Bartlett seems an acceptable appointment. He dies May 38, 1886.

31 Werne, *The Imaginary Line*, p 33.

32. Werne, *The Imaginary Line*, pp 47, 54.

33. Werne, *The Imaginary Line*, p 56.

34. Quoted in Werne, *The Imaginary Line*, p 56.

35. Werne, *The Imaginary Line*, p 213.

36. Mary Daniels Taylor, *A Place as Wild as the West Ever Was* (New Mexico State University Museum, 2004), p. 5.

37. Quoted in Taylor, *A Place as Wild as the West Ever Was*, p. 30.

38. It is likely that many or even most of these first 60 settlers were prior followers of Rafael Ruelas. Ruelas, who was born in 1816, is issued his own grant on January 4, 1848, southeast of downtown El Paso, on the Texas side of the border. This is just before the Treaty of Guadalupe Hidalgo is signed but after Doniphan has occupied El Paso del Norte. Ruelas and fellow settlers occupy the grant until August 1849 when an Indian raid kills at least 15 of the settlers. Ruelas leads his remaining followers to Doña Ana, and then on to the Mesilla site. He is appointed alcalde by Oritz, thus becoming the first mayor/justice of the peace of Mesilla. As alcalde, he co-signs the contract to build the church of San Albino. He is elected Justice of the Peace in the first election in Mesilla after it becomes U. S. territory. In 1855 he is elected to the New Mexico Territorial Legislature. He sells his grant claim in 1883. His grant is never recognized by the U. S. government. Ruelas dies in Mesilla on August 3, 1895.

39. John Russell Bartlett, *Personal Narrative of Explorations and Incidents in Texas, New Mexico, California, Sonora, and Chihuahua* (D. Appleton & Company, Vol 1, 1854), p 214.

40. Werne, *The Imaginary Line*, p 58.

41. Born October 26, 1826. After the Mexican-American war, Bull *"returning to Mesilla with a few hundred dollars, took a contract for sawing lumber for Fort Fillmore. ...one cold night while in the Organ mountains a lonely Indian came to his camp, cold and hungry.... [Bull gave him] coffee and tobacco.... This Indian turned out to be the chief of the Organ Mescalero tribe and returning with a few of his warriors he gave Bull to understand that his cattle would be protected by the Indians for his act of kindness."* (*Rio Grande Republican*, January 6, 1899) After Mesilla became U. S. territory, Bull moves back to the town and becomes a successful merchant and a large wine producer. He dies January 1, 1899, leaving 60,000 gallons of wine in his estate.

42. *"Mesilla vs. United States,"* Bull testimony. U. S. Court of Private Land Claims, Santa Fe, New Mexico, June Term, 1898. RG 49.3.4, National Archives and Records Administration (NARA).

43. *"Mesilla vs. United States,"* Bull testimony.

44. *Rio Grande Republican*, January 6, 1899

45. *"Colonization Regulations Issued by the Supreme Government of the State of Chihuahua, 22 May 1851."* *Executive Documents of the Senate of the United States*, Vol. 1581, 1873-74. Doc. No. 56, p 21.

46. Ortiz is a man of unusual background. He is born in Santa Fe in 1813 and educated in Mexico City. Appointed curate at El Paso del Norte on January 1, 1838. On November 5, 1841, a group of American prisoners who had been lead into New Mexico by General Hugh McLeod arrived in El Paso in seriously mistreated condition. Ortiz's generous aid to these prisoners is described by George W. Kendall in his book *Narrative of the Texan-Santa Fe Expedition.* *"Seldom have I parted from a friend with more real regret than with Ortiz, and as I shook him by the hand for the last time, and bade him perhaps an eternal adieu, I thought if ever a noble heart beat in man it was in the breast of this young generous priest."* (Kendall). When Doniphan occupies El Paso del Norte, he takes Ortiz captive, considering him a dangerous anti-American agitator. On leaving the city, Doniphan takes him hostage. Ortiz is well treated while a prisoner, having his own carriage. Following Doniphan's victory at the Battle of Sacrament, Ortiz is released. After his activity as Immigration Commissioner in 1851-53, he returns to his duties as priest and does not serve again in political office. He dies March 11, 1896.

47. *Executive Documents of the Senate of the United States,* Vol. 1581, 1873-74. Doc. No. 56, p 21, 26; Fidelia Miller Puckett, *"Ramon Ortiz: Priest and Patriot,"* New Mexico Historical Review, Vol. XXV, October, 1950, p 280.

48. Ortiz to Uribes, Doña Ana County Deed Records, Book B, p 237.

49. Ortiz to Ruelas, Doña Ana County Deed Records, Book B, p 231

50. Ortiz to Uribes, Doña Ana County Deed Records, Book B, p 237

51. *"Mesilla vs. United States,"* Bull testimony.

52. Born September 10, 1819. Bean is with Doniphan as a member of Company A, 1st Missouri Mounted Volunteers during the Mexican-American War. He recalls the following about that time: *"In December, 1846, the United States troops went into El Paso [del Norte], and were quartered in the rooms where the public records were kept; and it was very common to light the candles and kindle the fires with the papers in the rooms; we were quartered in El Paso about two months, and I frequently saw leaves of the records taken whenever any paper was wanted for any purpose."* (Quoted in *Executive Documents, House of Representatives,* 1856-57 Doc. No. 73. p 43.) Following the war, he returns to New Mexico, working as a teamster. On March 11, 1849, he marries in El Paso del Norte. In September, 1854, he is elected the second sheriff of Doña Ana County, the first of 5 terms. He dies October 29, 1903.

53. Bean testimony, *U. S. Court of Private Land Claims,* Santa Fe, New Mexico, June Term, 1898. RG 49.3.4, National Archives and Records Administration (NARA).

54. John B. Colligan and Terry L. Corbett, editors, *1851 Census of La Mesilla,* from Juarez Municipal Archives (Libro 243, f. 195-230). The census reports 37% are married individuals, 20% are youths, 23% are single, 14% are children, and 6% are widowers (categories include both sexes).

55. *"Mesilla vs. United States,"* Exhibit B, *Mesilla Civil Colony Grant,* U. S. Court of Private Land Claims, Santa Fe, New Mexico, June Term, 1898. RG 49.3.4, National Archives and Records Administration (NARA).

56. *Sheboygan Lake Journal,* June 29, 1853.

57. Werne, *The Imaginary Line,* p 142.

58. Werne, *The Imaginary Line,* p 193.

59. *Historical Sketch of Governor William Carr Lane,* Ralph E. Twitchell, (Historical Society of New Mexico. 1917), p 18

60. *"William Carr Lane, Diary,"* Edited by Wm. G. B. Carson, New Mexico Historical Review, 39, July 1964, p 217.

61. George Griggs, *History of Mesilla Valley or the Gadsden Purchase, Known in Mexico as the Treaty of Mesilla* (Bronson Print Company, 1930), p62; *New York Daily Times,* May 31, 1853; *Washington Union,* June 5, 1853.

62. Werne, *The Imaginary Line,* p 176.

63. *Executive Documents of the Senate of the United States,* Vol. 1581, 1873-74. Doc. No. 43, p 18.

64. Werne, *The Imaginary Line,* p 178.

65. *Democratic Banner,* August 5, 1853.

66. Exhibit A, *Executive Documents of the Senate of the United States,* 1873-74. Doc. No. 56, p 16.

67. Griggs, *History of Mesilla Valley or the Gadsden Purchase, Known in Mexico as the Treaty of Mesilla,* p 85.

68. The county of Doña Ana is established by the Territorial Legislature on January 6, 1852. The first county seat is the town of Doña Ana. The seat is moved to Las Cruces from Jan 1, 1853 to Dec 31, 1855. On Jan 1, 1856, the seat is moved to Mesilla.

69. Cuentas Azules is one of the signatories of a peace treaty with the United States on July 1, 1852. The treaty was ratified by the U. S. Senate March 23, 1853. Charles J. Kappler, *Indian Affairs: Laws and Treaties,* Vol. II, 1904.

70. Azules buys a horse from a soldier at Fort Fillmore who previously had bought the horse from Borule. Borule claims Azules stole the horse. On November 6, 1853, Borule finds Azules in a drunken stupor at Doña Ana and clubs him to death. *Daily Illinois State Register,* February 9, 1854; *Daily Missouri Republican,* March 30, 1854; Richard Wadsworth, *Forgotten Fortress* (2002), pp 109-110.

71. Werne, *The Imaginary Line,* p 181.

72. Utley, *Changing Course,* p 29.

73. *New York Daily Times,* June 6, 1853.

74. Werne, *The Imaginary Line,* p 185.

75. Werne, *The Imaginary Line,* p 186.

76. Utley, *Changing Course,* p 31.

77. *The New Volumes of the Encyclopedia Britannica,* (10th Edition 1911), p 732.

78. Born about 1802. Cubero is listed in the 1851 Mexican census as married but with no wife present. He is granted a farm lot by Ortiz. He is the Prefect of Mesilla in 1853 when Miranda divides Mesilla and Santo Tomas de Yturbide. In 1855 he is elected as Doña Ana County's representative to the fifth Territorial Council (Senate). He is elected again the following year. He dies March 3, 1869.

79. Wadsworth, *Forgotten Fortress,* p 129.

80. *Brownstown Jackson County Democrat,* February 6, 1855.

81. Meriwether is appointed to replace Lane on May 6, 1853. General John Garland is military commander of New Mexico.

82. For some unexplainable reason, Bennett provides the wrong date for this event. The date he gives cannot be right as extensive primary sources support the November 16, 1854, date and contradict Bennett's date of July 4, 1855. *"James A. Bennett Diary,"* New Mexico Historical Review 22, April, 1947, p 166; *Philadelphia Inquirer,* January 5, 1855.

83. *Philadelphia Inquirer,* February 1, 1855.

84. Wadsworth, *Forgotten Fortress,* p 132.

85. *"James A. Bennett Diary,"* New Mexico Historical Review, p 166.

Mesilla 1856-1865

The goal of this chapter is to reconstruct Mesilla, circa 1856-1865.

Mesilla Townsite

When Rafael Ruelas leads his 60 settlers from Doña Ana to Mesilla, he is well-aware of the challenges, having established a colony once already. His first official responsibility is to allocate land, which requires laying out property lines. He believes he's settling in the United States. The standard United States allotment of land to settlers is 160 acres, established by the 1841 Preemption Act, which, as Thomas Bull testifies, is how Mesilla is surveyed initially.[1] Perhaps Ruelas and some of his

The Mesilla townsite fits into a 960 x 960 varas block, 160 acres. The old section of Mesilla fits into a 960 x 320 varas block, 53.3 acres. The section marked off in the upper left corner is the "California Section."

men do the first surveying, or perhaps a dragoon from those stationed at Doña Ana does it.

If you take a satellite image of Mesilla today and fit a 960-by-960-varas block around it (160 acres), you get the image shown on the prior page. Mesilla fits into the 160 acres, although as a parallelogram rather then a square, indicating, perhaps, the surveying is done by chain or rope rather than by instruments.

Calle del Norte (North Street) is the north border, Calle del Sur (South Street) the south border, Avenida de Mesilla the east border, and Calle del Oeste (West Street) the west border.[2]

The old part of Mesilla fits nicely into a 960-by-320-varas parallelogram, which is the size of the blocks that Ortiz allocates originally, 53 1/3 acres.

The irregularly shaped block in the upper left corner of the townsite is the *"California section."* The south border of this section is an acequia originally called the California acequia. The section probably gets it name because Calle de Norte is the original road to California.[3]

Street Names

The street names used in Mesilla today are not the names assigned to the streets prior to about 1890. It is assumed by several writers that the streets had Spanish names originally, and those names are evidence of Mesilla's legacy as a Mexican colony. Not true. The early deeds only name a few streets, but those they do name have English names.

The most important street in the early years, and the site of the town's major businesses, is *"Main Street."* Today this street is Calle Principal. Calle Principal is the street running along the west side of the plaza. Main Street is the only street ever referred to by name in the Mesilla newspapers.

The street on the east side of the plaza, called today Calle de Guadalupe, is *"Second Street"* in the early deeds.

The street one block east of the plaza, Calle de San Albino today, is called both *"First Street"* and *"East Street."*

Avenida de Mesilla is called *"the road to El Paso."*

The streets that run east-west are unnamed. The street running along the north and south sides of the plaza are described as such, for example *"the street leading from the north east corner of the plaza."* The other east-west streets are simply called *"a street"* or *"a cross street."*

La Iglesia de San Albino

Various authors have speculated that San Albino was originally located south of the plaza. There is no evidence of this in the deed records. The most commonly suggested location for an *"original"* church is the block immediately south of the plaza, known as the Overland Stage block, but the property deeds fully account for the owners of that block with no sign of church ownership.

There also is no evidence of the existing church block being purchased in the deed records. When Las Cruces is laid out by Lieutenant Sackett, a church lot is allocated, which is the norm for Western towns at the time. These arguments convince the author that the Mesilla church was always located on the block where it is now.

In April, 1855, the officials of Mesilla let a contract to build the first San Albino:

"We, the citizens Rafael Ruelas and Cesario Duran, as commissioners named by all the people of this place of la Mesilla in order to begin to build a church on this plaza, have entered into an agreement with the Citizen Bonifacio Gamboa by which he will build such an edifice contracting for it, and taking it upon himself to finish it for the amount of nine hundred pesos in money, and the measurements of which church and the other conditions are as follows: It ought to be 30 varas in length; 15 varas in width, inside measurements; it should be 5 and one half varas in height, covered on the inside with mescla [plaster], the people giving the lime; it should have two towers of two parts, supporting the hewn poles upon which the bells will be hung: the foundations have to be of stone, the residents furnishing this: For the completion of said church the said Bonifacio has established the end of December of the present year, a time which he has considered sufficient."

"Also the said Bonifacio will be obliged to build a sacristy joined to the same church, the residents supplying the adobes which will be needed. All the other necessary things, doors, windows, vigas, tacote [thatch], for the said church should be supplied by the residents. It is also required that the church should have three naves, the floor being brick, and the towers also of brick. In witness whereof, and the fulfilling of all that is contracted, we offer this present document, signed in la Mesilla, today, the 15th of April, 1855."

"[signed]
Bonifacio Gamboa
Rafael Ruelas
Cesario Duran" [4]

By 1906 the original San Albino is in bad condition, so Father Grange contracts for a new church building, which is completed in 1908.[5]

Plaza

The plaza is another block for which there is no deed. It, too, is undoubtedly laid out in the initial survey. Incontrovertible evidence of this is that many of the deeds for terreno de solars (house lots) specify that the lot is adjacent to the "public plaza."

Thomas Bull in his Federal Court testimony makes a statement about the plaza that is confusing but probably means that neither Ortiz nor Miranda issued a deed for the plaza:

"Question: Do you remember whether Miranda set off a public square or plaza?"

"Answer: No, I do not recollect about that. I do not recollect. I hardly believe that either of them [Ortiz or Miranda] did give a public square there. I have no recollection of there being set off a public square." [6]

Maurin-Leonard Block

The block west of the plaza is the site of the Maurin-Leonard store. The block is also called the Barela Block.

The Maurin-Leonard block, west of the plaza.

Lot A: The original owner is Juan Jose Lopez who has a store and winery on the property. He sells to Antonio Constante on September 18, 1863.[7] Constante also uses the property for a store.

Lot B: The first owner is unidentified, but by 1859 it belongs to Marcos Apodaca who has a dramshop on the property.[8]

Lot C: By April, 1854, this is the site of a store and dramshop owned by Mariano Ysejara.[9] He is likely the first owner. During the Confederate occupation of Mesilla, troops are stationed here. By 1863, the lot is owned by Maria Rafaela Barela, divorced wife of Anastacio Barela.[10]

Lot D: Originally owned by Pedro Perez and his wife, who have a store on the lot.[11] Pedro appears in the 1851 census and is one of the administrators of the Mesilla Civil Colony Grant. In 1857 he splits his lot and sells the plaza-facing portion to Charles A. Hoppin and Nathan Benjamin Appel who open a store and dramshop.[12] [13] In 1858, Perez and his wife sell the remaining portion of their lot to Hoppin and Appel.[14] In 1859, Hoppin and Appel sell both lots to Alexander Duval, who continues to operate a store on the property. In 1863, Duval sells to Joseph Reynolds and James Edgar Griggs, who establish the firm of Reynolds & Griggs on the property.[15] [16]

Lot E: The first owner is Juan Pablo Albillas, who receives the lot as a grant. By 1857, Albillas sells to Augustin (Aguste) Maurin. In a legal dispute, Maurin, through his lawyer, claims to own the property from before September 25, 1853, but that seems to be a false claim.[17] On acquiring the property, Maurin enters into a partnership with Eugene Leonard, a fellow Frenchman, in the firm of Leonard & Maurin, a trading, freighting, and mining business.[18] In 1860, Maurin, after firing the bricks himself, builds a brick structure on the lot.[19] The original plan is for a two-story building, but Maurin seems to have built only half of the second story.[20] Leonard leaves the partnership in 1862, fleeing the Union occupation of Mesilla.[21] On April 9, 1866, Maurin is brutally murdered in his house by thieves searching for money and valuables assumed to be hidden in the building.[22] [23]

Hayward-McGrorty Block

This block is named after Hayward and McGrorty, merchants and freighters. It is south west of the plaza. The block today is mostly vacant with none of the first structures still standing, yet this was the second most important block in Mesilla after the Overland Stage block. The businesses on these blocks faced each other, opening onto Main Street.

Lot A: In 1856, Bautista Montoya has a dramshop on this lot.[24] In 1859, he sells the lot to Numa Grandjean, a Swiss immigrant, who opens a store on the property.[25] Some time after 1880 it becomes the property of Demetrio Chavez.

Lot B: Granted to Cristobal Ascarate, who has a dramshop here as early as 1854.[26] He still owns the property in 1880. Some time after 1910 it was purchased by John and Otto Bombach, who establish a store on the property.

Lot C: Juan Marolin is probably the original owner. He is certainly the first to build on the property, erecting an *"adobe house containing a store room and dwelling houses."* In 1857, he sells the lot to Rosa Lopez.[27] In 1860, George A. Hayward and William McGrorty[28] acquire the property for their firm Hayward & McGrorty. *"Messrs. Hayward & McGrorty, wholesale merchants, are also erecting a large and commodious store on Main street, opposite the Overland Mail office. In the rear of the store they are also building a large warehouse."* [29] On April 13, 1863, their property is seized by Marshal Abraham Cutler,[30] based on a charge of treason against the United States for aiding the Confederacy. Cutler sells the property to John Lemon in a public auction.[31]

Lot D: The original owner is unknown. In 1861, Guillermo Lopez sells the property to Robert H. Cochran.[32] Cochran establishes Cochran & Co on the property, *"offering a fine assortment of goods, embracing every thing needed in the trade."* [33] Business must have been worse than expected, as 13 months later, Cochran sells to James Edgar Griggs for only $100.[34] Thomas Bull buys the property a few years later for a residence and store.

Lot E: By 1860, this property is owned by Pinckney R. Tully.[35] The prior owners are unknown. Father Jose de Jesus Baca acquires the property in 1864. In 1866, Francis Blake acquires the property, divides the lot into two pieces, and establishes a flour mill on the back piece along the acequia madre.[36]

The Hayward-McGrorty block, south west of the plaza.

Lot F: Owned by Llagasta Joseph "Jose" Alert[37] as early as 1856, who has a dramshop on the property.[38] Alert is an avid supporter of the Confederacy. When he learns that Union troops are approaching Mesilla, he sells to Jacob Applezoller.

Overland Stage Block

This block is named after the Southern Overland Mail and Express Line. It is south of the plaza.

Lot A: The original owner is unknown. Samuel "Sam" Bean[39] acquires the lot about 1859. He sells it to his brother Roy Bean in May, 1862.[40] On April 13, 1863, after Roy Bean is convicted of treason, Marshal Cutler confiscates the lot and sells it in a public auction to John Lemon and John N. Hinckley.[41] Lemon sells it to Hinkley a month later.[42] Hinkley holds it for 2 years, sells it to Albert C. Gould[43], who then sells it back to Lemon.[44] Lemon opens a store on the property and is living there when he is killed in the Mesilla Riot.[45]

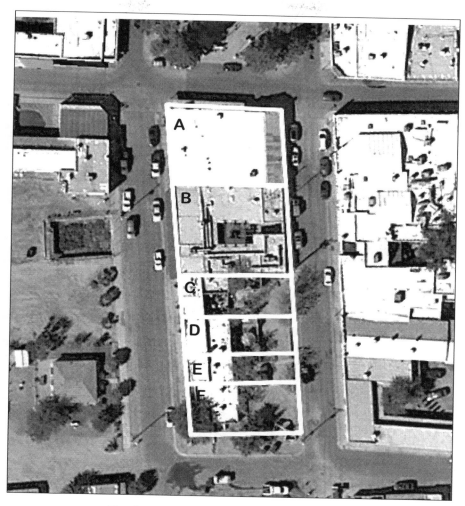

The Overland Stage block, south of the plaza.

Lot B: Anastacio Ascarate receives the lot as a land grant. On June 12, 1858, he sells to Joshua S. Sledd. The lot contains *"a large adobe house built in the form of a hollow square... fronting to the west side on main street"* [46] Sledd installs a billiard table and operates the property as a hotel, saloon, and store, called the Casino Hotel. *"If you want to lounge an hour, drop in at SLED's and take a game of Billiards, and a glass of native wine. (none of your drugged stuff.) Next door he keeps all the articles of merchandise usually kept for this market."* [47] Sledd also hosts the courthouse until it is built in 1868 and provides a deliberation room for the jury.[48] A list of Sledd's property in 1869 includes: *"2 billiard tables with 34 billiard balls, 24 cues, 2 bridges, and 2 tackers; bar fixtures, including a clock, 1 dozen decanters and 2 dog bar glasses; 1 pool table and 16 balls; 20 large looking glasses; and 8 bedsteads and beds."* [49] Under later owners, this property becomes the Mesilla Hotel and the Oliver Saloon.

Lot C: Granted to Rafael Armijo[50] who runs a store and dramshop on the property. He is sued and convicted on May 27, 1857, by the County of Doña Ana for *"maintaining a public nuisance [at his store and house] in the form of broken adobes and often rubbish in the street obstructing its passage, etc ."* [51] In April, 1863, he is convicted of treason and his properties in Mesilla and Las Cruces are confiscated by Marshal Cutler. Besides the properties, Cutler confiscates $19,812 in goods and $38,964 in cash.[52] Pinckney R. Tully and Stephen Ochoa buy this lot from Marshal Cutler on April 13, 1863.[53]

Lot D: This and Lot E are the location of the Southern Overland Mail and Express Line. On June 22, 1859, Giles Hawley superintendent and agent of the Overland Mail Company buys the property from Eugene Leonard and Augustine Maurin.[54] Following the start of the Civil War, the U. S. Government orders the Overland Mail Company to liquidate its business in the South.[55] On May 18, 1861, Owen Tulles, superintendent of the Overland Mail Company, sells the property to George H. Giddings.[56]

Lot E: On December 9, 1859, Giles Hawley buys this lot from Vincent St. Vrain and Amelia St. Vrain.[57] On May 18, 1861, Owen Tulles sells the lot to Giddings.[58] Giddings establishes the San Antonio-San Diego Mail Line in the two properties. In July 7, 1866, Frank DeRyther[59] acquires both lots D and E.[60]

Lot F: The original owner or owners are unknown. In 1859, the property is owned by Charles A. Hoppin. By August, 1861, Hoppin sells to DeRyther, who opens the Ten Pin Alley, a saloon and bowling alley, on the lot. A few years later, DeRyther opens the Texas Pacific Hotel on this lot. In 1866, when he acquires lots D and E, he expands the hotel into those properties. He pays taxes that year for a saloon, eating house, and billiard table.[61]

La Posta Block

This block is named after La Posta. It is the block south east of the plaza.

Lot A: The site of La Posta. The ownership chain of this lot is documented in the next chapters. The first owner is Nestor Varela, who owns the property by at least 1859.

Lot B: Granted to Juan Jose Duran. Duran sells it to Marcelino Gallegos[62] on April 9, 1854, who opens a dramshop.[63] In 1869, Gallegos sells the east half of his lot to Lola Bennett, owner at the time of the La Posta lot.[64] Gallegos retains the lot until he dies in 1911.

Lot C: Granted to Jesus Biescas.[65] In 1859, Biescas sells to Charles A. Hoppin and Nathan B. Appel. On April 27, 1861, Hoppin and Appel sell to Joshua S. Sledd.[66]

Lot D: Andres Vega owns the lot in 1861. Prior owners are unknown.

Rest of block is vacant prior to 1862.

The La Posta block, south east of the plaza.

Courthouse Block

The Courthouse block is the block east of the plaza, the block on which the Doña Ana County courthouse and jail will be built in 1867. Billy the Kid is imprisoned in the jail and tried, convicted, and sentenced to hang in the courthouse, in April, 1881.[67]

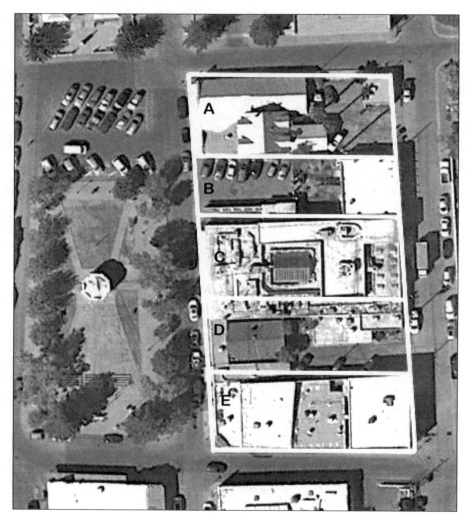

The Courthouse block, east of the plaza.

Lot A: Granted to Mateo Guerra, who is listed in the 1851 census and said to be the first resident on the plaza.[68]

Lot B: Granted to Juan Guerra, who may be Mateo Guerra's father. The intervening owners are unknown, but by 1877, it is purchased by Morris Frudenthal, who establishes a store on the property.[69]

Lot C: Granted to Faustino Mease. Next owner unknown.

Lot D: On October 21, 1854, Valentin Maese and Eulogio Baldoñado sell this lot to Louis William Geck,[70] which makes Geck the first non-Hispanic to own property in Mesilla.[71] A "Balentin Maes" is in the 1851 census, so Maese is likely the original owner. Geck opens a store on the property, which is a branch of the large store he operates already in Doña Ana. When the Union occupies Mesilla, Geck is accused of treason by Marshal Cutler and jailed for one year. His store is confiscated and used to quarter Union troops. When the occupation of Mesilla is lifted, the building and interior of his store are damaged so extensively that Geck sells the property. Nepomunceno Y. Ancheta buys the lot and building in late 1863 and opens a dramshop and store.[72]

Lot E: This is the lot on which the courthouse will be built. The original owner is unknown. On October 30, 1859, Narcisso Balencia and Ramon Gonzalez sell to Zenobio Madrid.[73] Madrid sells to Nestor Varela who sells to Sam Bean on March 13, 1862.[74] Sam has his house on the west half of the property and corrals on the east half. After Sam Bean is accused of treason, Marshal Cutler confiscates the property and on July 18, 1864, sells the property to Frank Higgins and Francis Blake.[75] In 1867, the Mesilla commissioners obtain the property and build on it a courthouse and jail. No deed has been found for this transaction.

The River

Until 1865, the Rio Grande River runs between Las Cruces and Mesilla, a significant barrier to travel between the two towns:

> *"During the months of May, June, July, August and September, the river is not fordable; first, it is swelled by the melting of the snow on the Rocky Mountains; after that, comes the season of rains, which begin in August, and continue through three months. During this stage of high water emigrants have to make rafts to cross on, or risk their animals by swimming; while equestrians cross in a canoe, their horses or mules swimming along side."* [76]

Even when the river is low, the bosque lining it was often marshy, or when dry, sandy and silty, making it difficult to cross.

In 1862, the Rio Grande breaks out of its bed and floods vast areas of the Mesilla Valley, including the east portion of Mesilla. When the flood recedes, the river returns to its original banks.

But in March, 1865, the river breaks out again:

> *"The Rio Grande is very high and slowly but continually rising. It is now within twelve inches of the highest point reached in 1862. On the third the river broke through the levee between the towns of Mesilla and Pica-*

cho, and on the eleventh broke through in a second place near Picacho. It is impossible to stop these crevasses, and the water has spread over a considerable portion of the valley destroying many large and small farms. The town of Mesilla is now on an island, and not accessible except by boats. The river bids fair to form a new channel at the foot of the Mesa Lands, leaving Mesilla on the east side of the river." [77]

The rampage continues:

"The Rio Grande has not been satisfied with ruining wheat and corn fields along its borders, but has entered several towns, has driven the population into the hills, and has washed away houses with everything they contained. The towns of La Mesa and Sabinal below, and Padillas, Pajarito and Atrisco above Las Lunas have met with the worst fate in this regard." [78]

Brigadier General James E. Carleton, military commander of New Mexico, in traveling from Franklin, Texas, to Las Cruces writes the following about the flood:

"On the way thither I found that the Rio Grande had risen higher than ever before known, from the melting of the immense fields of snow in the Rocky Mountains at its source. The past winter had been more severe than any other known or written about since the settlement of this country; and the melting of the accumulated snows increased the volume of water in this river to a corresponding extent. You are doubtless aware that most of the cultivated fields of this territory lie along the river and are irrigated by its waters. Thus when the great flood came, a great many of those fields were entirely washed away by the force of the current cutting new channels for the river, or were submerged and crops drowned. Many towns were injured and some villages entirely destroyed, the people living in them being obliged to abandon them and move from the valleys to the hills."

"When I arrived at Las Cruces..., I found great suffering for want of food – and was obliged to give the people subsistence stores, or see them literally starve to death. In addition to the calamity of the flood, came two insects which attacked the wheat and then myriads of grasshoppers, and finally, in the Mesilla Valley, there came the most fearful hailstorm ever known, which ruined in that locality all the crops that had escaped the scourges named." [79]

When the flood recedes, the Rio Grande is flowing in a new channel, on the opposite side of Mesilla, where it is today.

Timeline

- October 21, 1854 – Geck buys property in Mesilla
- April 15, 1855 – Contract given to build San Albino church
- March 23, 1857 – Hoppin and Appel established
- June 12, 1858 – Sledd establishes Casino Hotel
- June 22, 1859 – Overland Mail buys first lot
- December 9, 1859 – Overland Mail buys second lot
- 1860 -- Hayward & McGrorty established
- 1860 -- Augustin Maurin builds brick building west of plaza
- April 12, 1861 – Civil War begins with attack on Fort Sumter
- May 18, 1861 – Overland Mail sells properties
- August, 1861 – DeRyther establishes the Ten Pin Alley
- 1863 – DeRyther establishes the Texas Pacific Hotel
- November 3, 1863 --Reynolds & Griggs established
- March 11, 1865 – Rio Grande breaks out of old channel
- April 9, 1866 – Maurin is murdered

Photos

On the left, the Mesilla plaza with the San Albino bell tower visible above the trees. On the right, the Corn Exchange/La Posta building (foreground) and the Courthouse (the street is between the buildings). Circa 1900. Courtesy Archives and Special Collections, New Mexico State University.

Looking at San Albino from the east along what is now Calle De Santiago. Circa 1900. Courtesy Archives and Special Collections, New Mexico State University.

On the left, the Courthouse Block. The closest building is Lot A. On the right the
Mesilla plaza with the Overland Stage Block visible at the far end. Circa 1900.

Looking across the plaza at the Courthouse (with the porch) and La Posta blocks. Circa 1910. Courtesy Palace of Governors Collection.

On the left, the Hayward-McGrorty Block. On the right the Overland Stage
Block. The new San Albino visible in the distance. Circa 1908.

Looking south. On the left, the Overland Stage Block (the Saloon is in the old Overland Stage offices). On the right the Hayward-McGrorty Block. Notice the Hayward-McGrorty Block has been completely rebuilt since the photo taken in 1908 shown on the previous page. The second building behind the Chaves Grocery Store is the Bombach store, built after 1914. Courtesy Palace of Governors Collection.

The Maurin-Leonard Block. Circa 1915. Courtesy Palace of Governors
Collection.

The Maurin-Leonard Block. Note that the plaster applied to the Maurin building. Circa 1920. Courtesy Palace of Governors Collection.

The Overland Stage Block. Circa 1924. Courtesy Palace of Governors
Collection.

Courthouse Block, courthouse at right. Circa 1924. Courtesy Joe Lopez.

Looking at the courthouse building on the Courthouse Block, with the corner of the La Posta building just visible. Circa 1929. Courtesy Joe Lopez.

Footnotes

1. *"Mesilla vs. United States,"* Bull testimony.

2. The Mesilla deeds with very few exceptions refer to north, south, east, and west boundaries, even though the town is actually oriented along a north-east, south-west axis. This book follows the same convention.

3. This book will not detail the original owners of lots in the California section, a favorite location of the Mesilla wealthy in the years after the Civil War.

4. Mary Taylor papers, translation by Mary Taylor, NMSU Archives and Special Collections, Ms 0162. The first priest was Father Bernardino Hinojos, the second Jose de Jesus Cabeza de Baca.

5. See Chapter 1.

6. *"Mesilla vs. United States,"* Bull testimony.

7. Juan Jose Lopez to Antonio Constante, September 18, 1863, for $560.34, Book 1, p 31. Constante was a Peruvian who was operating a freight train into the Mesilla valley as early as 1852-53.

8. Doña Ana County Probate Book A, Doña Ana County Courthouse.

9. Doña Ana County Probate Book A.

10. Anastacio Barela, born 1827, is already a wealthy merchant and freighter when he arrives in Mesilla in 1854. He is a strong supporter of the Confederacy and flees Mesilla ahead of the Union occupation. Before leaving, he divorces his wife, Maria Rafaela Garcia, and places this property in her name, possibly to protect the property. He is indicted for treason and Marshal Cutler confiscates and sells his other properties. He dies September 15, 1878. Maria Rafaela Barela dies May 27, 1915.

11. Doña Ana County Probate Book A.

12. Pedro Perez and Ysidra Garcia to Charles A. Hoppin and Nathan B. Appel, March 23, 1857, for $450. Book B, p 367.

13. Charles A. Hoppin comes to Mesilla from Franklin, Texas, where he is a judge. In 1858, he is appointed postmaster of Mesilla. His wife, who he marries after arriving in Mesilla, dies soon after the marriage, probably in childbirth. Shortly before he dies on January 31, 1864, he asks his friend Pinckney R. Tully to care for his son. Tully adopts Charles, giving him the name Charles Hoppin Tully. Nathan B. Appel comes to New Mexico in 1847 as an employee of Tully. In 1852, he establishes a store in Las Cruces. Two years later he moves his business to Tucson, Arizona. In 1858, he moves to Mesilla and establishes the partnership with Hoppin. The partnership is dissolved with the selling of their Mesilla property and Appel moves to Tubac, Arizona. Appel dies January 5, 1901.

14. Pedro Peres and Ysidra Garcia to Charles A. Hoppin and Nathan B. Appel, February 15, 1858, for $60, Book B, p 368.

15. Alexander Duval to Reynolds & Griggs, partners, November 3, 1863, for $800 Book 1, p 48.

16. Joseph Reynolds is born Februry 25, 1825, in Ireland. He dies January 10, 1883. See note 2, Chapter 4. For details on Griggs, see note 2, Chapter 4.

17. Letter to Brigadier General West, Commanding, District of Mesilla, from Frank Higgins (Maurin's attorney), regarding Maurin's property, December 31, 1863.

18. Doña Ana County Probate Book A.

19. *Mesilla Times*, October 18, 1860.

20. The one-and-a-half story brick building still stands, and is considered to be the oldest extant brick building in New Mexico.

21. See Chapter 3.

22. Augustin Maurin probate file, Doña Ana Courthouse.

23. Maurin's murderers are never caught. At the time of his death, he has almost 22,000 pounds of copper ore and 8,000 unused bricks in his home. Maurin's brother Cesar Maurin inherits the property. Twenty-eight years later, Pedro Duhalde, the owner of the property then, is brutally murdered in the building by thieves looking for hidden wealth. Those murderers, too, are never caught.

24. Doña Ana County Probate Book A.

25. Bautista Montoya to Numa Grandjean, March 13, 1859, for $50, Book B, p 515; 1860 census.

26. See note 14, Chapter 3.

27. Juan Marolin to Rosa Lopez, March 16, 1857, for $388, Book B, p 264.

28. Hayward is born in 1826. Following service in the Mexican-American war, he makes his way to Fort Fillmore, where he serves as the first postmaster in 1852. There he meets William McGrorty, born 1824, in Ireland. The two are already established merchants and freighters when they open their store in Mesilla, having owned the sutler store at Ft. Fillmore. Both are ardent supporters of the Confederacy. Faced with the imminent occupation of Mesilla by Union troops, Hayward and McGrorty liquidate as much of their assets as they can. On February 14, 1862, they sell a freight train of 10 wagons and 100 mules for $11,000 in Confederate vouchers and a $1,000 note. After leaving Mesilla, Hayward fights for the Confederacy, rising to the rank of Lt. Colonel under General Stevenson. McGrorty undertakes a secret mission for Colonel John Robert Baylor, commander of the Confederate forces at Mesilla, to travel to New York and cash Union vouchers and checks discovered at Fort Fillmore after its abandonment by the Union. McGrorty carries out this dangerous assignment successfully, cashing all but one check, and sending the money by carrier to the Confederate Government at Richmond, Virginia. Hayward dies in 1903, McGrorty in 1904.

29. *Mesilla Times,* October 18, 1860.

30. See Chapter 3 for details on Marshal Cutler.

31. U. S. Marshal Abraham Cutler to John Lemon and John N. Hinckley, April 13, 1863, for $750, Book 1, p 239

32. Guillermo Lopez to Robert H. Cochran, March 24, 1861, for $188.92, Book C, p 6, mortgage with payment due in December.

33. *Mesilla Miner,* June 9, 1860.

34. Robert H Cochran to James Edgar Griggs, April 6, 1862, for $100, Book C, p 160.

35. Born March 25, 1824. Tully is a merchant in Santa Fe as early as 1847. In 1851, he builds a magnificent, 10-room home in Santa Fe that still stands and is a public museum. In 1860, when he opens his store in Mesilla, it is just a branch of his merchant empire which extends from Santa Fe to Tucson, Arizona. He dies November 10, 1903.

36. The mill owners are Daniel Frietze, John Lemon, and Francis Blake; Pinckney R. Tully and wife to Francis Blake, January 5, 1866, for $500, Book 3, p 245. The mill had been established originally at a different location by Robert P. Kelley and was both steam and water driven. It was acquired by Lemon in a bankruptcy sale.

37. Born in Spain in 1826. In January, 1860, the county commissioners authorize Alert to rent and collect fees for the use of the plaza. In the months before the Civil War begins, Alert is one of the major advocates of Southern sentiment in Mesilla. He dies in 1907.

38. Doña Ana County Probate Book A.

39. See note 52, Chapter 1.

40. Samuel G. Bean to Roy Bean, May 4, 1862, Book C, p 154.

41. US Marshal Abraham Cutler to John Lemon and John N. Hinckley, April 13, 1863, for $260, Book 1, p 243.

42. John Lemon to John N. Hinkley, July 2, 1863, for $130, Book 1, p 128.

43. John N. Hinckley to A. C. Gould, August 2, 1864, for $1450, Book 1, p 130.

44. Albert C. Gould to John Lemon, November 22, 1864, for $1,600, Book 3, p 457.

45. Born 1831. Lemon is in Mesilla by 1860. He is one of the few supporters of the Union in Mesilla. After the Confederate occupation of Mesilla, he is accused of spying and imprisoned for almost one year. On February 18, 1862, Lemon and fellow Union supporters Crittenden Marshall and Jacob Appelzollar are taken from jail at night by a rogue group of Confederate soldiers led by Ammon Barnes, who intends to execute them. They are taken to a large cottonwood tree, where Marshall is hung. Lemon is next, but while they are putting the rope around his neck he starts making Masonic signs. One of the Confederate

soldiers, a fellow Mason, demands that he be saved, and the rope is removed. Appelzollar begins begging for his life, but is strung up anyway. After he passes out, he is cut down and resuscitated. (Notes by Katherine Stoes; Lemon testimony in Ammon Barnes Libel trial.) Lemon buys almost all of the Mesilla property confiscated and sold by Marshal Cutler. On August 27, 1871, during a political riot on the Mesilla plaza, Lemon was struck on the head by a heavy club. Taken to his house, Lemon is told by his physician that he is dying. He calls for his attorney, and in the presence of Appelzollar and other witnesses, dictates a verbal will: *"I give all my property to my wife. Every thing I possess I wish her to have. Every thing belongs to her. She will pay my debts."* He dies shortly thereafter.

46. Joshua S. Sledd to Marcelino Gallegos, November 22, 1869, for $1, Book 4, p 25.

47. *Mesilla Miner,* June 9, 1860.

48. Doña Ana County Probate Book A.

49. Joshua S. Sledd to Marcelino Gallegos, November 22, 1869, for $1, Book 4, p 25.

50. Born 1815. Rafael Armijo is a nephew of General Manuel Armijo, the last Mexican governor of New Mexico. He and his brother Manuel are wealthy Albuquerque freighters and merchants before the Mexican-American War. When Rafael is granted his house lot in Mesilla, he already has a store in Las Cruces. He is a strong supporter of the Confederacy and one of their major suppliers during their occupation of Mesilla. By one account, he loans the occupation government $400,000, which he never recovers. He flees Mesilla prior to the Union occupation and never returns. In 1865, President Andrew Johnson issues Armijo a Presidential Pardon for his conviction for treason. He dies May 15, 1887.

51. Doña Ana County Probate Book A.

52. *"The Exploitation of Treason,"* Edward D. Tittman, New Mexico Historical Review 4, 1929. pp 128-45.

53. Abraham Cutler, Marshal, to P. R. Tully and S. Ochoa, April 13, 1863, for $175, Book 1, p 24.

54. Eugene Leonard and Augustine Maurin to Giles Hawley superintendent of the Overland Mail Company, June 22, 1859, for $800, Book B, p 428.

55. The Civil War is generally considered to begin with the attack on Fort Sumter on April 12, 1861.

56. Owen Tulles superintendent of the Overland Mail Company to George H. Giddings, May 18, 1861, for $1,500, Book B, p 666.

57. Vincent St. Vrain and Amelia St. Vrain to Giles Hawley, superintendent and agent of the Overland Mail Company, December 9, 1859, for $600, Book B, p 410.

58. Owen Tulles superintendent of the Overland Mail Company to George H. Giddings, May 18, 1861, for $1,500, Book B, p 666.

59. Born about 1823. DeRyther comes to Mesilla as an employee of the Overland Mail Company. He dies June 22, 1870.

60. G. H. Lyon to Frank DeRyther, July 7, 1866, for $1200, Book 3, p 186.

61. Record of New Mexico Territorial Taxes, 1866, Ancestry.com.

62. Born about 1834. Gallegos serves several times as Justice of the Peace. He dies February 28, 1911.

63. Juan Jose Duran to Marcelino Gallegos, April 9, 1854, for $50, Book B, p 525.

64. Lola Bennett to Marcelino Gallegos, July 29, 1869, Book 3, p 536. See Chapter 3 for details.

65. Charles A. Hoppin and Nathan B. Appel to James J. Webb and John M. Kingsbury, mortgage for $1300, Santa Fe, N. M., November 1, 1859. Some sources say this lot is used as the headquarters of the Confederacy during its occupation of Mesilla. Not true. The headquarters was located on Colonel John Baylor's lot in the California Section of Mesilla.

66. Charles A. Hoppin and Nathan B. Appell to Joshua S. Sledd, April 27, 1861, Book 4, p 25.

67. Billy is captured by Sheriff Pat Garrett on December 23, 1880, and taken to jail in Santa Fe. After a change of venue request by the District Attorney Rynerson, trial is ordered in Mesilla. He is taken from Santa Fe to Rincon by train, and from Rincon to Mesilla by wagon, arriving in Mesilla on March 28, 1881. He is charged with the murder of two people, Andrew L. "Buckshot" Roberts and Sheriff William

Brady. The case against him for the killing of Roberts is dismissed due to lack of jurisdiction – but it is unlikely he would have been convicted of murdering Roberts, not being guilty of that killing. He is convicted of killing Brady on April 9, 1881, and sentenced to hang on April 13, 1881. Because the scene of the crime is Lincoln, New Mexico, he is ordered to be hung there. He leaves Mesilla on April 16, 1881, chained in a wagon and under heavy guard, and arrives at Lincoln on April 21. He escapes from jail in Lincoln on April 28, 1881, 15 days before he is to hang, killing two guards to do so. Garrett kills him at Fort Sumner on July 14, 1881. See note 63, Chapter 3.

68. Taylor, *A Place as Wild as the West Ever Was.*

69. Bernard Weisl to Morris Frudenthal and wife, Oct 1, 1877, for $1000, Book 5, p 79.

70. Valentin Maese and Eulogio Baldonado to Louis William Geck, October 21, 1854, for $80. Book B, p 258.

71. Born June 4, 1818, in Poland. Geck arrives in Doña Ana in 1848 as a dragoon. After mustering out, he quickly becomes a successful merchant. In 1862, Marshal Cutler accuses him of treason, jails him without a trial, and confiscates his properties in Doña Ana, Las Cruces, and Mesilla. When he is tried finally in 1863, he is acquitted and his property is returned. He sues the U. S. Government for damages to his Mesilla property, asking $1,700, but apparently he receives no compensation. He dies June 9, 1890.

72. Doña Ana County Probate Book A.

73. Narcisso Balencia and Ramon Gonzalez to Zenobio Madrid, October 30, 1859, for $1500, Book B, p 424.

74. Nestor Barela and wife to Sam G. and Roy Bean, March 13, 1862, price not given. Book C, p 130.

75 Abraham Cutler, Marshal, to Frank Higgins and Francis Blake, July 18, 1864, for $60. Book 1, p 44.

76. *Sacramento Daily Union,* February 11, 1858.

77. *Santa Fe Weekly Gazette,* May 27, 1865. Quoted in *"A Historical Study of Floods Prior to 1892 in the Rio Grande Watershed,"* a thesis by Rufus H. Carter, Jr., NMSU, 1953.

78. *Santa Fe Weekly Gazette,* June 17, 1865. Quoted in *"A Historical Study of Floods Prior to 1892 in the Rio Grande Watershed."*

79. Letter by James E. Carleton, Brigadier General, Comanding, New Mexico, July 9, 1865, to the Adjutant General United States. Quoted in *"A Historical Study of Floods Prior to 1892 in the Rio Grande Watershed."*

Chapter 3 | Corn Exchange Hotel

Property History

The first known owner of the La Posta lot is Nestor Varela.[1] He is in Mesilla as early as September, 1855, when he serves as an election judge.[2] It is unclear if he owns the property then, but he certainly does by 1859 when he pays license fees for a mercantile store and dram shop.[3] On February 6, 1862, he enters into a co-partnership agreement with Sam and Roy Bean.[4] For $1,000 he sells them half of his merchandise and property and gives them full management of the firm.[5]

On March 6, 1862, he sells the other half of his business to Sam and Roy for $2,000.[6]

Roy sells his share of the business to Sam on May 6, 1862. Sam runs the business under the name Samuel Bean & Co.[7]

On February 19, 1863, Sam Bean's property is confiscated by U. S. Marshal Abraham Cutler.[8] [9] The basis for this seizure is the Confiscation Act of 1862. Passed by Congress and signed by President Lincoln on July 17 of that year, the law has two major provisions: it frees slaves in Confederate territory occupied by the Union and permits the seizing of any and all property owned by U. S. citizens who aid the Confederacy by action or by material support.[10]

Mesilla had been occupied by Confederate soldiers on July 25, 1861. The overwhelming sentiment in Mesilla among the Anglos and wealthy Hispanics in the town is pro-Confederacy, and the Confederates are warmly welcomed. Later that day there is a battle between Union troops from Fort Fillmore and the Confederates on the southern outskirts of Mesilla, which is won handily by the Confederates (the Battle of Mesilla). This defeat causes the Union forces to abandon Fort Fillmore in an extremely ill-considered and disorderly attempt to retreat. The Confederate forces pursue and capture the fleeing Union soldiers without a fight, putting southern New Mexico and Arizona into Confederate hands.[11]

In response, the Union solicits volunteers in Southern California, eventually mustering a force of about 2,500 men. By July 1862, these men, calling themselves the *"California Column,"* are approaching Mesilla, following an arduous forced march overland. The occupying Confederate soldiers and their civilian supporters decide to abandon Mesilla. On August 7, 1862, Mesilla is formally occupied by the First California Cavalry, led by Lt. Col. Edward E. Eyre.[12]

Propelled by strong anti-Confederate sentiment, New Mexico Marshal Cutler and the judiciary in Santa Fe move quickly to apply the Confiscation Act. U. S. citizens accused of aiding the Confederacy are denounced in a legal process known as a Libel. In theory a Libel requires the testimony of two witnesses to convict a defendant, but one witness is the usual practice and even that is waived in a few cases.

The Libel defendants are not represented in person or by counsel, having fled New Mexico with the Confederates.[13]

In Sam Bean's case, one witness testifies against him, Cristobal Ascarate.[14] He testifies that Bean served as both justice of the peace and marshal under the Confederates, and sold them, among other things, ten wagons and 60 mules.[15]

Bean is convicted and the court authorizes the confiscation of his property. Marshal Cutler sells Bean's La Posta lot to Leopoldo Carrillo in a public auction on the Mesilla plaza on April 13, 1863.[16] Unusual for the time, the house on the lot is described as a stone building, not an adobe building.[17]

The Confiscation Act offers marshals selling confiscated property broad opportunities for corruption, including rigged sales. In October, 1864, Cutler is charged with gross embezzlement for collecting over $52,000 in fees in his confiscation actions in New Mexico. He is acquitted by a jury in a trial in 1867.[18]

On April 2, 1866, Carrillo sells the house and lot to John Lemon.[19]

Lemon holds the lot until December 25, 1867, when he sells to Lola Bennett.[20] Lola[21] is the wife of Joseph F. Bennett[22], a California Column veteran. The Bennetts (Lola by some accounts) build a new structure on the lot, evidently removing the stone structure.

Looking for space to expand, Lola buys half of her southern neighbor's lot for $125.[23] The seller is Marcelino Gallegos. The half-lot he sells is vacant, but he occupies the half he keeps. To obtain the lot, Lola must agree to certain restrictions:

> *"Lola Bennett hereby agrees that in erecting buildings or stables upon that portion of a lot that was purchased by her from Marcelino Gallegos she will not cause any doors or windows to be put in on the side opening into the corral of Marcelino Gallegos, nor any corrals conducting water from the roof of such buildings or stables into the corral of Marcelino Gallegos. But it is expressly understood that in erecting buildings or stables upon the premises, she reserves the right to put into any such buildings or stables any ventilators on the side adjoining the corral of Gallegos that she may deem necessary."* [24]

The Bennett's initially use their new home as a store. In 1869, they pay $25 in taxes on $500 worth of merchandise.[25]

In June of 1870, Frank DeRyther,[26] owner of the Texas Pacific Hotel and the Overland Stage property dies. This provides an opening for Bennett, who by July, 1870, has the mail contract for the Mesilla to Santa Fe run and is operating the Southern Overland Mail and Express Line, based in the old Overland Mail property.[27]

The 1870 census shows Joseph Bennett living on the La Posta lot, with Lola and their son Cortland (age 3), two domestic servants, and William Keegan, mail conductor, Phillip Hartz, mail conductor, and John Long, stage driver.[28]

John "Jack" Davis

In May, 1874, the Bennett's trade their La Posta property for a lot and house in the California section[29] of Mesilla:

"John Davis and Col. Bennett changed residences. Col Bennett is well-pleased with his orchard and gardens, and Mr. Davis is preparing his house, which is on the corner of the plaza, to keep a saloon, billiard room and gentlemen's club rooms, which will be kept as only 'Jack' Davis knows how." [30]

Davis has been in Mesilla since 1863, after mustering out of the California Column. He makes his living first as an auctioneer, then as a liquor distributor. In 1870 he becomes a stage driver, riding for Bennett's Southern Overland Mail and Express Line.[31] On March 1, 1873, Davis marries Agustina Castillo.[32]

In August, 1873, Davis gets into a squabble with the political leaders of Mesilla, who are Republican. Davis, a Democrat, feels that the county convention to elect state representatives is rigged. He stands up and challenges the chair, Pablo Melendrez. After increasingly heated verbal exchanges between the two men, Melendrez orders the sheriff to remove and jail Davis. The result:

"Mr. John Davis, who was so badly beaten by Sheriff Barela last Sunday, that he has been confined to his bed, is said to be recovering, but his collar bone being broken, it will be long before he is entirely well. If Mr. Davis had no rights at a convention called as a mass convention by our Probate Judge, or if his motions and inquiries were calculated to disturb the harmony of said mass convention – why, Mr. Barela perhaps had no other recourse but to shut down on free speech and teach people a lesson.... But every thinking citizen asks if it was necessary or right, for the Sheriff of this county, when he had a citizen locked in a cell of the jail to open that cell for the purpose of knocking down the prisoner, with the butt of his pistol, and then when down, stamping him until his body was most severely bruised and his bones broken." [33]

Davis' purpose in trading for the La Posta lot is to open a saloon and restaurant, which he announces to the public on May 30, 1874:

"CORN EXCHANGE"

"From the first of June 1874, this Saloon will be open to the public, at the Corner of the Plaza, opposite the Court House. The Bar room with a reading and other apartments for gentlemen and customers, have been newly and nearly refitted. The best qualities of the best kind of Liquors and Cigars will be kept at the Bar. The proprietor will spare no pain to make his establishment first class in every respect. The strictest order will be enforced at all times, so that no gentleman shall be in any manner annoyed. The patronage of friends and customers is solicited."

"John Davis, Proprietor" [34] [35]

The reviews are celebratory:

"The Corn Exchange: Under the Superintendence of our friend Mr. Fletcher Jackson continues to win encomiums from all. To any of those who hanker after a good meal properly served we commend the Corn Exchange Restaurant, while the Bar for the elegance of its appointments, and the excellence of the liquors with which it is supplied has no equal in this portion of the Territory." [36]

"John Davis, of the Corn Exchange Hotel, is ever ready and glad to see his hundreds of friends, as the latch-string hangs outside the door, and they have only to give it a jerk and walk in. His table is bountifully supplied with fruits, vegetables, etc., and the bar with lemons and everything else to be had." [37]

By September, 1874, Davis is calling his establishment the Corn Exchange Hotel. On the 2nd of that month, he orders a billiard table:

"The Corn Exchange Hotel is neatly and orderly kept by the prince of caterers John Davis, who has his table loaded with the best the market affords; the NEWS and other papers are found in the reading rooms; and his wines, liquors, cigars and lemons are not surpassed anywhere. Give him a call. Mr. Davis has bought a J. M. Brunswick & Balke Billiard table, and will soon have in position the finest billiard table in the territory." [38]

His food is lauded repeatedly. Here's why, almost unbelievable for Mesilla:

"The Corn Exchange Hotel, of which John Davis is proprietor, presents for to-morrow's dinner, Sunday, Sept 20, the following:

BILL OF FARE
SOUPS *-- Oyster, Ox-Tail, Vegetable.*
FISH *-- Catfish, Mackerel, and Whitefish, Boiled and Broiled.*
ROASTS *-- Pig, Beef, Veal, Lamb, Ox-Heart, Stuffed.*
BOILED *-- Mutton, Beef, Veal, Beef Ribs, Venison.*
SIDE DISHES *-- Boned Chicken, Chicken Pie, Ham, Boiled Tongue, Wine Sauce.*
VEGETABLES *-- Green Corn, Cabbage, Carrots, Tomatoes a la Tini-Pie, German Rice, Boiled Onions a la Crème, String Beans.*
RELESHES *-- Pickled Tongue, Cucumbers, Sardines, Pickled Beets, Jellies.*
PASTRY *-- Apple dumplings, Custard Pie, Grape Pie, Peach Pie, Transparent Pudding, Tarts, Cream Puffs.*
DESSERT *-- Raisins, Almonds, Filberts, Grapes, Peaches, Apples, Melons."* [39]

In response, the newspaper recommends people immigrate to Mesilla for the *"daily worship at the shrine of Epicurious dishes at the bountifully supplied table of the Corn Exchange."* [40]

As if the food is not enough draw, Davis puts up *"a sign, some twenty feet long.... It was painted by Jack Howland, and although he is a portrait painter, and makes no pretension to sign painting, yet we must say that, for a mingling of colors and neat, exquisite taste, this sign cannot be beat in the territory."* [41]

Davis' timing for opening a hotel could hardly be more opportune. Mesilla is booming. Mines in the Pinos Altos and Silver City area are producing huge quantities of gold and silver, and other minerals. Mesilla is the transshipment point for these metals, providing enormous stimulus to local businesses.

In May, 1874, *"$1,512, in gold dust"* arrives from Pinos Altos and *"$5,200 in bullion [comes] in from Silver City."* [42] Every coach brings in *"slabs of silver bullion."* On September 12, the stage leaves with *"between four and five thousand dollars in bullion."* [43] The next week, it carries $4,000 worth,[44] an action repeated almost every week for the next two years.

This stimulates nefarious interests, too. There are many stage robberies; the most famous, which makes even Eastern papers, occurs on January 12, 1876:

> *"About 3 [am] as the coach was coming from Silver City to Mesilla, three white men, masked with handkerchiefs... stepped out from behind the rocks, aimed their guns and revolvers at [the driver] and said: 'Get down... and don't move or we will shoot you.'"*

> *"There was in the coach at the time John S. Chisum, Esq., the 'Cattle King' of the West.... Mr. Chisum had $1,000 in greenbacks in his inside coat pocket, and while the silver bricks were being taken out, he kept taking from $100 to $200 at a time from his pocket-book, without taking it out from his pocket, and would scatter it around in the seat of his pants and drawers, leaving about $100 in the pocket-book."*

> *"One soon came, got the $100 and a very fine gold watch...."*

> *"They secured about $4,000 in silver bricks.... Three bricks were marked 'From H. M. Porter,' and three 'From J. F. Bennett,' and all addressed: Kountz Brothers, New York."*

> *"Just before the bandits left, Mr. Chisum said: 'I don't like to beg, but I wonder if you could please give me enough to buy grub with until I reach home?' The fellows gave him a dollar."*

> *"The robbers were tracked about forty miles to where the roads fork, one going to Mesilla and the other to Fort Seldon, both on the Rio Grande. The silver bricks weighted about 300 pounds, which must have been a pretty heavy load for the three horses to carry, besides their riders.... Suspicion is attached to certain persons, but we will not now mention any names, as it may interfere with certain plans laid to capture the three persons and recover the treasure."* [45]

Hotel Register

The Corn Exchange's Hotel Register has survived the travails of history. The book is a custom print job, with *"Corn Exchange Hotel Register,"* *"(JOHN DAVIS, Proprietor),"* and *"La Mesilla, New Mexico"* at the top of each page. The delay in getting the book produced probably explains why the first entry is August 31, 1875. Written on the flyleaf of the book and signed by A. Davis is:

"Steal not this book
for fear of shame
for in it you will
find the Owner's name" [46]

The names in the book, which are often in the handwriting of the guest, are a "who's who" of the residents of the Mesilla Valley. One of the right columns is used to record whether the guest has a mount. The nightly rent for a bed is $1. The rent for a bed and a horse or mule is $1.50.

The guests are virtually all men, with one entry for a woman without an accompanying man[47], and just several for a man and a wife. The usual accommodation is three to six guests a night, but one entry shows 17 guests. It is rare for a person to stay more than one night, but there a quite a few guests who stay regularly.

Guests come from as far away as London and Hong Kong, and cities like San Francisco, Denver, St. Louis, Chicago, New York, and Washington D. C.

On November 6, 1875, Samuel B. Axtell, Governor of New Mexico, stays at the Corn Exchange. On New Year's Eve, 1875, Davis writes this ditty in the Register:

"Farewell 'Old Year'
May all thy faults
And ill go with thee
And thy successor bring
Us much joys."

There is an entry for U. S. Grant, Washington City [D. C.], on November 18, 1875. This is not Ulysses Simpson Grant, who is president in 1875, but his son Ulysses Simpson Grant, Jr. No record of why Grant Jr. is in Mesilla has been found. Probably he is travelling to or from California on the stage. U. S. Grant [Jr] stays at the Corn Exchange again on June 12, 1876.

On January 12, 1876, is written *"Coach Robbed in Cooks Canyon Jany 12 1876,"* clearly referring to the stage robbery involving Chisum noted earlier. Under the date January 13, 1876, is written *"Three Thousand Dollars Reward Offered."* And below that, under the date January 14, 1876, is an entry for John Chisum of Bosque Grande, showing he stayed at the Corn Exchange that night. The same night there are entries for two U. S. army men, probably soldiers who participated in the hunt for the robbers.

Intriguing, but not surprising, are the number of hotel guests who are tied to Billy the Kid[48] and the Lincoln County War.[49]

Silver City Sheriff Harvey H. Whitehill stays in the Corn Exchange on November 7, 1875, the first of many times. This is just 6 weeks after he has arrested Billy the Kid for his first crime:

"Henry McCarty, who was arrested on Thursday and committed to jail to await the action of the grand jury, upon the charge of stealing clothes from Charley Sun and Sam Chung, celestials, sans cue, sans Josa sticks[50], escaped from prison yesterday through the chimney. It's believed that Hen-

ry was simply the tool of "Sombrero Jack," who done the stealing whilst Henry done the hiding. Jack has skinned out." [51]

When this theft is committed, Billy is 16 years old. After he escapes, he leaves his home in Silver City, never to return. Any reluctance to leave behind his stepfather and older brother Joseph is likely reduced by the earlier death of his mother of *"an affection of the lungs"* on September 16, 1874.[52]

Another frequent guest who will deal with Billy as sheriff is James Webster Southwick.[53] He is sheriff of Mesilla when Billy is tried for murder and sentenced to hang in Mesilla, on April 13, 1881.

A friend and accomplice of Billy who later becomes a bitter enemy stays many times at the Corn Exchange: John William Kinney, *"King of the Rustlers."* [54] He lists his residence as *"Kinney's Ranch."* John Kinney and Jessie Evans are the leaders of a gang of cattle and horse thieves known as the *"Boys."* A local newspaper describes the ranch as *"about three miles from town on the west bank of the river... the headquarters and rendezvous for all the evil doers in the county."* The article further states *"There are several grave accusations against some of these men [at the Ranch], one of them is wanted in Arizona...."* [55]

This man *"wanted in Arizona"* is almost certainly Billy. On August 17, 1877, Billy had killed Frank P. Cahill in what is likely self-defense:

> *"Henry Antrim shot F. P. Cahill near Camp Grant on the 17th inst., and the latter died on the 18th. Cahill made a statement before death to the effect that he had some trouble with Antrim during which the shooting was done. Bad names were applied to each other.... The coroner's jury found that the shooting 'was criminal and unjustifiable, and that Henry Antrim alias Kid, is guilty thereof.'"* [56]

This is the first documented mention of Billy as the *"Kid."* Billy flees before any trial, making him *"wanted."*

That Billy is riding with the *"Boys"* is clear by October 8, 1877:

> *"On Monday last, three horses... were stolen from Pass' coal camp in the Burro Mountains.... Sometime on Tuesday, the party of thieves, among whom was Henry Antrim, were met in Cook's canon by Mr. Carpenter...."*

> *"The thieves who stole the horses from the Burro Mountains last Monday, stopped the western bound coach 7 miles east of Fort Cummings, asked the driver if he 'had anything on,' and on his replying no, said, 'Well, we'll let you pass this time;' insisted on Morehead taking a drink with them and finally rode off after remarking that they were leaving the country. There was nine of them each armed with two revolvers and a Winchester rifle, and carrying two belts with cartridges."* [57]

The Lincoln County War, in which Billy will become a major participant, is raging at this time. There is no clear beginning of the War, because it grows out of on-going conflicts, but a possible date could be November 6, 1876, when the Englishman John Tunstall[58] arrives in Lincoln for the first time. Tunstall with his ambition and financial resources will be the catalyst for an explosion in violence that eventually ensnares up to 200 men and results in roughly 80 killings, including the one for which Billy is sentenced to hang.

On September 22, 1877, three men who will later be Billy's closest friends and allies in the Lincoln County War stay at the Corn Exchange: Josiah G. "Doc" Scurlock, Charles Bowdre, and Richard M. Brewer.[59] [60] They spent the previous three days chasing some of the *"Boys"* led by Jessie Evans. The gang had stolen several horses from Tunstall and Alexander A. McSween[61] on the 18th:

> *"This forenoon my horses and those of Mr. Tunstall were stolen from a ranche on the Rio Ruidosa.... Good citizens are in pursuit of the thieves and I hope they will overtake them and the plunder.... 'The Boys' are known."* [62]

Although the three pursuers caught up with the thieves at the San Augustin Ranch[63] the prior day, they are unable to recover the horses.[64]

Other people directly tied to Billy who stay at the Corn Exchange are: Attorneys Albert J. Fountain and John D. Bail, who defend Billy in his trial for the murder of William Brady; William Logan Rynerson, who as District Attorney relentlessly pursues the arrest and conviction of Billy, and blocks the territorial governor's attempt to grant Billy a pardon; Simon Bolivar Newcomb, the prosecuting District Attorney in Billy's murder trial; and Judge Warren Henry Bristol who sentences Billy to hang. Even William Brady stays at the Corn Exchange (on June 10, 1877), as do Billy's implacable enemies James J. Dolan and John H. Riley.[65]

Prank – Or Historic Event?

On page 31 of the Register, above the date March 15, 1876, is a scratchy signature that appears to be *"William Bonny."* Beside it in the Residence column is *"Fort"* and an unreadable word. The unreadable word, presumably the name of a fort, does not suggest any of the forts located in New Mexico or Arizona. At the top of the page, the same shaky hand apparently writes *"Thursday 16,"* meaning perhaps March 16, 1876 (see photo page 77).

Is the date credible?

Billy escapes jail and leaves Silver City on September 25, 1875. On August 17, 1877, he kills Cahill at Camp Grant. Billy's activities between these two dates are little known, although researchers have located personal accounts and reminiscences placing him in Arizona.[66] A recent writer has located more evidence that he spent this time in Arizona, including a document showing he was accused of stealing a horse at Camp Goodwin, Arizona, from Private Charles Smith on March 19, 1876.[67] This is three days after he "possibly" stayed at the Corn Exchange Hotel.

Thus, though it may be unlikely that he was in Mesilla on March 16, 1876, no currently-known evidence rules it out.

But there **are** strong reasons to doubt that Billy the Kid stayed at the Corn Exchange Hotel: the scratchy writing of the name, the unidentifiable residence, the use of the alias William Bonney, which Billy is not known to be using at this time, and the filling out of the date at the top of the page in the same handwriting. These facts suggest the entry is a prank, possibly by a child, given the almost undecipherable writing. A mitigating fact, however, is that the prankster, if he is such, has found a believable date and a blank space at the top of a Register page to put the signature.

No other page in the Register has blank space at the top of the page, so if the signature is added at a later date, the prankster found the only page where an entry could be added at that location, making the argument that the signature was written contemporaneously stronger than it would be if the signature was added at the bottom of a page.

To the author's eye, the ink appears to be very close in color to that used in the writing that follows *"Bonney's"* signature, and to have been made with a similar pen.[68]

Billy later wrote several letters to the Governor of New Mexico, Lew Wallace. How does his handwriting in those letters compare with that in the Register? An example of his signature is given on page 80. Look at the way the *"y"* is written. Does it resemble the *"y"* in the Register? What about the *"B?"*

Agustina Davis

On July 22, 1876, John Davis dies. He is 42 years old.[69]

Agustina takes over the operation of the Corn Exchange Hotel. There is no record of Davis' death in the Hotel Register[70], although guests are sparse for the week or so surrounding his death. The ads for the local paper now list A. Davis as the proprietor, and on some Register pages, *"John"* is crossed out and overwritten with *"Agustina."*

In February, 1879, the Corn Exchange hosts a billiard match:

> *"The new billiard hall at the Exchange Hotel was opened by a match game of one hundred points between Col. J. Howe Watts, of the Second National Bank, and Mr. R. Swartwout, of the Pay Department, on last Saturday evening, game commencing at 7 1/2 o'clock. The game was the three ball, French carom, and was closely contested to the end, being finally won by Mr. Swartwout -- score 100 to 67. The attendance was large and this really elegant little billiard parlor can be said to be fairly inaugurated."* [71]

No doubt large sums of money exchange hands that evening. A match of even greater significance follows:

> *"A billiard match of two games was played at the Exchange Hotel last Tuesday evening, between Mr. William H. Hayes, champion billiard player of Texas, and Paul Schwarze, one of the most prominent of our local billiard players. The first game was an American one of 170 points, and was won by Mr. Hayes, score, Hayes 170, Schwarze, 110. The second was the French three ball game, in which Mr. David J. Miller defended the amateur reputation of this ancient city, but he was defeated at last by the superior ivory punching of the gentleman from Texas. Mr. Hayes then gave an exhibition of fancy shots, and the entertainment closed."* [72]

Agustina decides apparently that she does not want to run the saloon, so on May 1, 1879, she leases it to W. R. "Doc" Simpson for one year, giving him the option to renew the lease yearly until 1884. The lease fee is $25 a month. The lease includes the following furnishings:

"Front room: 6 chairs, 12 chairs, 3 lamps, 1 settee, 1 table, 2 tables 'round'

Bar room: 1 block, 8 decanters, 6 bar spoons, 4 strainers, 3 waiters, 1 dice box, 1 looking glass, 1 book case, 1 pitcher, 1 cigar stand, 20 bar glasses

South room: Furniture complete

Parlor: bed and bedding, carpet etc, room pictures, 1 looking glass, mantle furniture, wash stand and its appurtenances, 1 lounge, 2 tables" [73]

The local newspaper notes the new management:

"Doc. W. R. Simpson, having leased the Corn Exchange Saloon has entirely refitted and refurnished the saloon and club rooms. He has a fine stock of good wines, liquors and cigars including some Old Medford rum, and brandy and whiskey that can't be beat. Mr. Ed Schwartz and Mrs. Simpson have arrived from Santa Fe; and "Ed" the popular mixologist guarantees satisfaction or no charge."

"Lunch tomorrow evening at 8:30 at the Corn Exchange. 'Ed' will 'dish up' anything called for." [74]

Ed is dishing up more than food at the Corn Exchange, however. On June 14, 1879, the *Mesilla News* reports in Spanish:

"There was a commotion this week involving the family of Doc Simpson at the Corn Exchange Hotel where employee Eduardo, according to some, made advances to his wife [Doc's]. Some violent threats followed and Eduardo and the Mrs. left to Las Cruces while Doc stayed at the saloon." [75]

In addition to losing his wife, Simpson appears to be a bad manager, perhaps a crooked manager:

"Doc. Simpson, a former saloon keeper in Santa Fe and lately in the same business in Mesilla, has skipped. He left numerous debts behind him and among others $3 for subscription to this paper. He said he was going to St. Louis. Family difficulties seem to have been the cause." [76]

Only one other reference to Doc Simpson has been located by the author, which places him in New York a few years later:

"'Doc' Simpson left this morning for Gouverneur, where he will 'tip' on the horse races during the fair." [77]

Following Simpson's exit, Agustina resumes managing the Corn Exchange herself. Ads for the hotel appear only rarely in the local newspapers, suggesting the Corn Exchange is in slow decline. For a while, part of the hotel is rented out as a dentist's office. In October, 1880, the *Thirty Four* prints the following:

"The attention of the local authorities is called to obscene pictures on exhibition in the saloon at the Corn Exchange Hotel in Mesilla, one of which is of a scandalous nature and so hung as to attract the attention of persons passing the door. Such exhibitions in the most prominent parts of the town should be forbidden, if there is any law to reach the case. We understand that this is only the beginning and that the same locality is shortly to be turned into a disreputable den of abandoned women. We hope our district attorney will find some law to prevent this. We believe that public sentiment in Mesilla will sustain any proper effort for the suppression of public immorality; and it is certainly the duty of every good citizen to discourage anything that tends to lower the standard of virtue in the community." [78]

The last reference to Corn Exchange Hotel in newspapers appears in March, 1882.[79] After that Agustina appears to have used the property only as a residence.

By 1883, Mesilla is being abandoned by most of her residents and businesses. In 1878, the Atchison, Topeka, and Santa Fe Railroad had announced plans to build a connecting railroad between Santa Fe and El Paso, Texas. The next year the company begins surveying the route the train will take through the Mesilla Valley. Mesilla and Las Cruces are both approached by representatives of the company soliciting land gifts to reduce the cost of building the line. The major businessmen and land owners of Mesilla strongly oppose any gifts, and apparently did not care to have the railroad pass through Mesilla. Las Cruces embraces the potential the railroad offers and town businessmen provide right-of-way and land for track and a city depot. The first train arrives in Las Cruces in late April, 1881.[80]

That same year, the New Mexico Territorial Legislature moves the county seat from Mesilla to Las Cruces. The Mesilla leaders fight this change, but unsuccessfully. Judge Bristol, who had sentenced Billy to hang, refuses for almost 12 months to approve the bond issue to build a new courthouse in Las Cruces, until overruled by a higher court.[81]

On November 25, 1908, Agustina dies. She and John had no children, so she has no direct heir. In her will, she disinherits two brothers, who are assumed to reside in Chihuahua, Mexico. She leaves her Corn Exchange property half to her friend Mrs. Antonia Provencio and half to the San Albino Church. She leaves a painting of John Davis to Mrs. Maria L. Montes. No trace of this painting exists today.[82]

She is buried in the Mesilla cemetery in an unmarked grave. It is reasonable to assume she is buried next to John Davis, but no record of her location exists. Her estate pays $5 for her coffin, $1 to have her grave dug, and $36 to San Albino priest Father Juan Grange for funeral expenses. Two doctors bill her estate a total of $98.80 for medical care in her final days.[83] She receives no obituary in the local paper, which by this time is based in Las Cruces.

Father Grange[84] buys the Corn Exchange property on March 14, 1909, for $805. After the expenses of the estate are subtracted, the proceeds are divided between Mrs. Provencio and the San Albino Church.[85]

Timeline

- July 25, 1861 – Confederates occupy Mesilla
- February 6, 1862 – Varela sells half of La Posta business/property to Sam and Roy Bean
- March 6, 1862 – Varela sells second half of La Posta business/property to Sam and Roy Bean
- May 6, 1862 – Roy Bean sells his share of La Posta business/property to Sam Bean
- July 17, 1862 – Congress passes the Confiscation Act of 1862
- August 7, 1862 – Union occupies Mesilla
- February 19, 1863 – Bean property confiscated by Marshal Cutler
- April 13, 1863 – Cutler sells La Posta property to Leopoldo Carrillo.
- April 2, 1866 – Carrillo sells La Posta property to John Lemon
- December 25, 1867 – Lemon sells La Posta property to Lola Bennett
- July 29, 1869 – Lola buys lot adjacent to La Posta property
- March 1, 1873 – Davis marries Agustina Castillo
- May, 1874 – Lola Bennett trades La Posta property to John Davis
- June 1, 1874 – Corn Exchange opens
- September 16, 1874 – Billy the Kid's mother dies in Silver City
- August 31, 1875 – First entry in Corn Exchange Hotel Register
- September 25, 1875 – Billy the Kid escapes jail in Silver City
- January 12, 1876 – *"Boys"* rob stage and passenger Chisum
- January 14, 1876 – Chisum stays at Corn Exchange Hotel
- March 16, 1876 – William Bonney "signature" in Corn Exchange Hotel Register
- March 19, 1876 – Billy accused of stealing horse from Private Charles Smith at Fort Goodwin, Arizona
- June 12, 1876 – U. S. Grant, Jr. stays at Corn Exchange Hotel
- July 22, 1876 – John Davis dies
- November 6, 1876 – John Tunstall arrives in Lincoln
- August 17, 1877 – Billy kills Frank Cahill at Camp Grant
- September 22, 1877 – Scurlock, Bowdre, and Brewer stay at Corn Exchange Hotel
- October 8, 1877 – Billy identified as riding with the *"Boys"*
- Early November, 1877 – Billy goes to work for Tunstall
- February 18, 1878 – Tunstall murdered.
- April 1, 1878 – Sheriff Brady killed.
- April 18, 1878 – Billy indicted for killing Roberts and Brady
- July 19, 1878 – Alexander McSween killed
- November 26, 1878 – Last entry in the Corn Exchange Hotel Register
- May 1, 1879 – Doc Simpson leases Corn Exchange saloon
- August 29, 1879 – Doc Simpson skips town
- April, 13, 1881 – Billy sentenced to hang by Judge Bristol
- April 28, 1881 – Billy escapes from the jail in Lincoln
- July 14, 1881 – Billy killed by Sheriff Pat Garrett
- November 25, 1908 – Agustina dies, wills Corn Exchange to Church and Mrs. Provencio
- March 14, 1909 – Father Grange buys Corn Exchange lot and building

Photos

Corn Exchange Hotel letterhead. Courtesy Special Collections, University of Arizona Library.

Corn Exchange Hotel advertisement. *Mesilla News,* September 12, 1874.

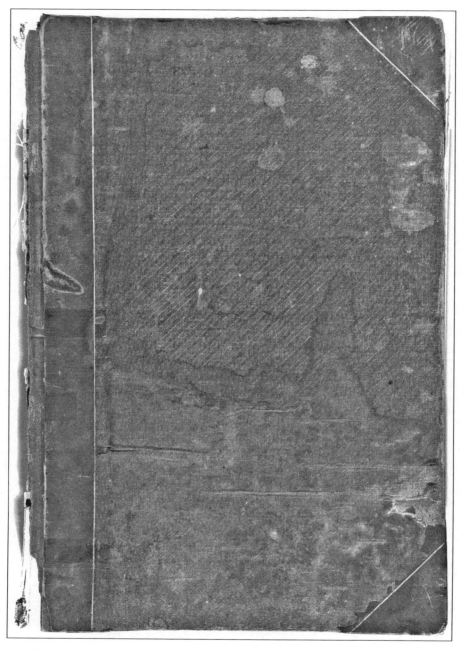

Corn Exchange Hotel Register. Courtesy Archives and Special Collections,
New Mexico State University.

Corn Exchange Hotel Register.

(JOHN DAVIS, Proprietor.)

La Mesilla, New Mexico, Wednesday, Nov. 3, 1875

13

NAME.	RESIDENCE.	Room.	Time.
Wednesday, Nov. 3. 1875.			
C. J. Dailey	Baltimore		5
Col. Wm. G. Boyle	London —	✓	6
Frank R. Anthony	Silver City	✓	5
W. P. Woods	Chicago	✓	5
Thursday, Nov. 4, 1875.			
F. C. Marsh	El Paso		5
A. Shutz	Las Cruces		5
John Kinney	Kinney's Ranch		
Friday, Nov. 5, 1875.			
Hon. Thos. B. Catron	Santa Fe, N. M.	} 2 Horses	
Judge S. B. Newcomb	Las Cruces, N. M.		
Saturday, Nov. 6, 1875.			
W. C. Waring	Gila Ranch	110	
D. Martin Chaves	City		5.
Gov. S. B. Axtell	Santa Fe		
Hon. Wm. L. Rynerson	Las Cruces,		
Judge Warren Bristol	City		
Hon. A. J. Fountain	"		
Ira. M. Bond	"		
Col. John Kinney	Kinney's Ranch		

Corn Exchange Hotel Register page, November 3-6, 1874. Guests include
John Kinney, Thomas B. Catron, Simon B. Newcomb, Governor Samuel B. Ax-
tell, William L. Rynerson, Judge Warren Bristol, and Colonel Albert J. Fountain.
Courtesy Archives and Special Collections, New Mexico State University.

Corn Exchange Hotel Register.   27

(JOHN DAVIS, Proprietor.)

La Mesilla, New Mexico, Jany 8th 1876

NAME.	RESIDENCE.	Room.	Time.
L. Bennett	Osborn M̅o̅		
Co. Goldsmith	City		
B. F. Chamberlain	St. Paul Minn	Jany 1̲2̲
Coach Robbed in Cogo's Canyon Jany 12 1876			
E. P. Keelner	Fork Selden N M		

Friday Jany 13th 1876

E. P. Keelner	Fork Selden W M		
Saml Lynn	Cummings N M		
Three Thousand Dollars Reward Offered			

Saturday   January 14th 1876

John S. Chisum	Bosque Grande		
A. S. Towar	U. S. Army		
R Swartwout	do		

Tuesday Jan 18th 1876

| Geo. Kennard | | | |
| S. M. Pomeroy | Saco City Maine | | |

Wednesday Jany 19th 1876.

| John W. Selden | St Louis Mo | | |
| C. Shurty | Julian Cal | | |

Friday Jany 22d 1876,

| J. M. Ginn | 73 | | |

Corn Exchange Hotel Register page, January 8-22, 1876. Notation on stage robbery, $3,000 reward, and John S. Chisum's registration. Courtesy Archives and Special Collections, New Mexico State University.

Corn Exchange Hotel Register.

(JOHN DAVIS, Proprietor.)

La Mesilla, New Mexico, *March 5th 14,* *1876*

NAME.	RESIDENCE.	Room.	Time.
William P. Bray	*Fort W. Engineroute*		
Wednesday March 15th			
Henry Benke	*St Louis Mo*		
H. A. Wells	*Saint Louis*		
Sunday March 26th 1876			
Jno Ryan	*Santa Barbara*		
Michael Manning	*Santa Barbara*		
Lito Garcia			
O. W. Keesey	*Fort Davis Texas*		
John Kinney			
F. H. Cooper			
Monday 27th Mar 1876			
S. R. DeLong	*Camp Bowie Apache Pass A T*		
Tuesday, April 8th 1876			
Judge G. al Drane	*El Paso*		
E. H. Jennings	*Washington D C*		
Monday April 9th			
Mrs Dr. Jessop	*Fort Selden*		
Mrs Capt. Carl	*do*		
H. L. Schaffer	*do*		
Tuesday April 10th 1876			
A. H. Morehead	*Silver City*		
Charles Evans	*do*		

Corn Exchange Hotel Register page, March 15–April 10, 1876. Apparent signature of William Bonney. Courtesy Archives and Special Collections, New Mexico State University.

Corn Exchange Hotel Register page, September 22, 1877-January 26, 1878.
Josiah G. "Doc" Scurlock, Charles Bowdre, and Richard M. Brewer stay at the
Hotel. Courtesy Archives and Special Collections, New Mexico State University.

Corn Exchange Hotel Register.

Agustina (JOHN DAVIS, Proprietor.)

La Messilla, New Mexico, 187

NAME.	RESIDENCE.	Room.	Time.
Wednesday June 12:			
James Dolan	Lincoln N.M.		
Jack Long	" "		
James West	Tularosa		
Doc Blazer	" "		
Gallegos	Santa Fe		
Sam Rayland	Cal.	5	
Rigby.	Silver City	5,00	
Thursday 13			
Martin Hoover	New York	114	
John Riley	Lincoln		
Friday 14.			
H.C. Haring	Minister to Canton		
George Ackenback	Las Cruces		
Manuel Flores	" "		
Saturday 15			
Chas Kirby	El Paso Tex		
C.N. Bennett	Silver City		
J.A. Tays	El Paso Texas		
Sunday 16			
J.D. Bail	Silver City		
E.J. McGinn	" "		
E.J. Rose	" "		
H.H. Whitehill	" " Dead beat		

Corn Exchange Hotel Register page, June 12-17, 1878. This pages shows a number of participants in the Lincoln County War: James J. Dolan, Jack [John] Long, James West, Joseph H. "Doc" Blazer, John Riley, John D. Bail, and Harvey H. Whitehill. Whitehill may have left without paying, given the *"Dead beat"* notation. Note *"John Davis"* is crossed out and *"Agustina"* written in. Courtesy Archives and Special Collections, New Mexico State University.

Billy the Kid's signature on a letter to New Mexico Territorial Governor Lew Wallace, March 2, 1881. Courtesy Indiana Historical Society.

Billy the Kid's "signature" on the Corn Exchange Register. Courtesy Archives and Special Collections, New Mexico State University.

Close-up of Billy the Kid's "signature" on the Corn Exchange Register. Courtesy Archives and Special Collections, New Mexico State University.

John Davis' grave, Mesilla Cemetery.

Footnotes

1. Born 1828, his name is written as both Varela and Barela. He is not listed in the 1851 Mesilla census.

2. *Miscellaneous Documents of the House of Representatives,* 34th Congress, 1856. Document No. 15. *"Case of Miguel A. Otero Contesting Jose M. Gallegos September 18, 1855,"* p 38.

3. Doña Ana County Probate Book A, Doña Ana County Courthouse.

4. See note 52, Chapter 1. Roy Bean, Sam's younger brother, is born in 1825. He joins Sam in Mesilla in 1855, after numerous scrapes with the law and several questionable killings. A strong Confederate, he flees Mesilla in advance of the Union occupation. He later becomes famous as Judge Roy Bean, *"Law West of the Pecos"* in Langtry, Texas. He dies March 16, 1903.

5. Nestor Varela with Sam G. and Roy Bean, February 6, 1862, Book C, p 140.

6. Nestor Barela and wife to Samuel G. and Roy Bean, March 6, 1862, Book C, p 95.

7. Roy Bean to Samuel G. Bean, May 5, 1862, Book C, p 158.

8. Testimony in libel case against Samuel and Roy Bean, February 19, 1863. RG 21, Civil and Criminal Cases, National Archives and Records Administration (NARA), Denver, Colorado.

9. Cutler is appointed U. S. Marshal for New Mexico on August 16th, 1862, and serves until January 26, 1866.

10. *Statutes at Large, Treaties, and Proclamations of the United States,* Vol 12, 1863, pp 589-92. The Confederacy also had confiscation acts to legitimize seizing the property of Union supporters in Confederate areas.

11. Jerry D. Thompson, editor, *New Mexico Territory During the Civil War* (2008), pp 2-3.

12. Thompson, *New Mexico Territory During the Civil War,* p 9.

13. *"The Exploitation of Treason,"* Edward D. Tittman, New Mexico Historical Review 4, 1929, pp 128-45.

14. Born 1818 in Janos, Mexico. Ascarate is one of the original colonists in 1850. His daughter marries James Edgar Griggs. He dies November 7, 1915.

15. Testimony in libel case against Samuel and Roy Bean, February 19, 1863.

16. US Marshal Abraham Cutler to Leopoldo Carillo, April 13, 1863, for $300, Book C, p 215.

17. Testimony in libel case against Samuel and Roy Bean, February 19, 1863.

18. *"The Exploitation of Treason,"* Tittman, pp 128-45.

19. Leopoldo Carrillo and wife to John Lemon, April 2, 1866, for $900, Book 3, p 465.

20. John Lemon and wife to Lola Bennett, December 25 1867, for $1,000, Book 3, p 529.

21. Born in September 29, 1846, Delores Lola is the daughter of John Patton, said by many sources to be the first American to come into New Mexico. She marries James on February 14, 1864. Her father dies March 13, 1866, and she probably inherits the money she uses to buy the La Posta lot. She dies in 1922 in Mexico City.

22. Born November 11, 1830. Bennett enlists in Company I, 1st infantry, California volunteers on August 18, 1861. He dies July 8, 1904, in Mexico City.

23. Marcelino Gallegos and wife to Lola Bennett, July 29, 1869, for $125, Book C, p 534.

24. Lola Bennett to Marcelino Gallegos, July 29, 1869, Book 3, p 536.

25. Record of New Mexico Territorial Taxes, 1868, Ancestry.com.

26. Born 1823. DeRyther first comes to Mesilla as a driver for the Overland Stage; founds the Ten Pin Alley and Texas Pacific Hotel; buys the Overland Stage properties in 1866; and is the Mesilla postmaster from 1862 to 1869. Dies June 22, 1870.

27. *Denver Rocky Mountain News,* July 9, 1870.

28. U. S. Census, New Mexico, 1870, taken September 6, 1870.

29. See Chapter 2.

30. *Mesilla News,* May 9, 1874. Bennett does not stay in Mesilla long. By October 12, 1875, he moves to Silver City and becomes heavily involved in mining. A year later he renames his stage line as the Bennett Line.

31. Record of New Mexico Territorial Taxes, 1864-68, Ancestry.com; U. S. Census, New Mexico, 1870, taken September 6, 1870.

32. San Albino Basilica, marriage records.

33. *The Borderer,* August 16, 1873.

34. *Mesilla News,* May 30, 1874.

35. "Corn Exchange" is a common name for hotels in the West. The first Corn Exchange is opened in London in 1747, and is named after the traders congregating in the area to trade Corn contracts. Hand-Book of London, 1850; The Leisure Hour, 1856. Quoted at victorianlondon.org/buildings/cornexchange.htm.

36. *Mesilla News,* June 27, 1874.

37. *Mesilla News,* August 29, 1874.

38. *Mesilla News,* September 2, 1874.

39. *Mesilla News,* September 19, 1874.

40. *Mesilla News,* October 3, 1874.

41. *Mesilla News,* October 3, 1874.

42. *Mesilla News,* May 30, 1874.

43. *Mesilla News,* September 12, 1874.

44. *Mesilla News,* September 26, 1874.

45. *Daily Inter Ocean,* February 5, 1876; *Las Vegas Gazette,* Jan 22, 1876. Smelters made silver bars heavy as a deterrent to stealing. Note that three of these bars belong to Joseph Bennett. The robbers are never caught.

46. Corn Exchange Register, MS 0080, NMSU Special Collections.

47. Mrs. Christian Duper and her 4 daughters, of Las Cruces, with 2 horses.

48. An immense amount has been written about Billy the Kid. It's unclear exactly when he was born. Almost all historians agree the year is 1859, the place New York City. His mother is Catherine McCarty. It's unclear if she is married to Billy's father, or even who his father is, when Billy is born as Henry McCarty or William Henry McCarty. Catherine marries William Henry Harrison Antrim in the First Presbyterian Church of Santa Fe, New Mexico, on March 1, 1873. This provides Billy with another name he often uses, William Antrim. For reasons unknown, he also refers to himself as William Bonney.

49. Lincoln County War – named after Lincoln County, New Mexico.

50. *"Celestials"* refers to Chinese. *"Sans cue"* means no long hair.

51. *The Grant County Herald,* September 26, 1875.

52. *Mining Life,* September 19, 1874.

53. Born April 21, 1843. Southwick is Mesilla postmaster from 1876 to 1881. In 1880 he is elected Mesilla sheriff. He dies March 23, 1922.

54. Born August 31, 1848. In late June, 1878, Kinney arrives in Lincoln at the head of 15 hired gunmen known as the *"Rio Grande Posse,"* to fight on Murphy-Dolan side of the Lincoln County War. Kinney is present during the 5-day war in Lincoln when McSween is killed and Billy just escapes with his life. He is indicted for his actions in Lincoln, but never tried. Oddly enough, Kinney is back on the law's good side by April 16, 1881. On that day he is deputized and serves as one of six guards transporting Billy

from Mesilla to Lincoln, to hang. Billy is *"hand-cuffed and shackled and chained to the back seat of the ambulance [wagon]."* The trip takes five days and Kinney is paid $2 a day for his services, receiving payment for both the trip to Lincoln and the return to Mesilla. In February, 1881, after he nearly beats one of his men to death, the local paper publishes a poem about him:

"There is a man in our town
And he tells wondrous lies
He carries 'round a six shooter
To pop out folk's eyes.

Now, why he is allowed to stay
I really do not know
But the cry is daily gaining ground
'The Rustlers must go!'"

A few weeks later the same paper publishes another Kinney poem. Has a gunman ever inspired so much poetry?

"Kenneyville [Rincon]

Who took those cattle?
I, said 'honest John,'
That's what I'm on,
And I took those cattle!

Who'll arrest John Kinney?
I, said Tom Coyn,
With this gun of mine,
I'll arrest John Kinney!

Who'll try the rustler?
I, said Judge Bristol,
If you'll take off his pistol,
Then I'll try the rustler!

Who'll catch his pals?
I, said Van Patten,
With this sword and baton,
I'll catch his pals!

Who'll prosecute them?
I, said Judge Newcomb,
Just let one or two come,
And I'll prosecute them!

Who'll dig their graves?
I, said Major Fountain,
In the side of a mountain,
I'll dig their graves!"

On March 8, 1883, Kinney is captured after an extensive manhunt. He is sentenced to five years in the New Mexico penitentiary, serves three, and is released. He dies August 25, 1919.

55. *Mesilla Valley Independent,* July 21, 1877.

56. *The Grant County Herald,* September 1, 1877.

57. *Mesilla Valley Independent,* October 13, 1877.

58. Born March 6, 1853 in east London, England. John Henry Tunstall is sent to Canada in September, 1872, to manage a branch of his father's business. Convinced that he can become wealthy in the United States, he leaves Canada in February, 1876, and travels to California looking for that opportunity. His search leads him to Lincoln on November 6, 1876, where he gets into immediate financial and political conflict with the people who dominate that part of New Mexico, the Murphy-Dolan faction. He is mur-

dered in cold blood on February 18, 1878. The murderers are well-known, but protected by dubious legal cover and the power of the Murphy-Dolan side. The killing of Brady for which Billy is sentenced to hang is part of an effort to obtain "citizen's justice" for Tunstall's killing. In the various movies on Billy the Kid, Tunstall is portrayed as an older, fatherly figure, but he is just 25 when killed.

59. Billy goes to work for Tunstall in November, 1877, having switched sides from the *"Boys"* and their allies Lawrence G. Murphy, James J. Dolan, and John H. Riley in early November.

60. "Doc" Scurlock survives the Lincoln County War and moves to Eastland, Texas, where he dies July 25, 1929. Charles Bowdre fires the shot that leads to "Buckshot" Robert's death, for which Billy the Kid is indicted, the case being dismissed at trial. Bowdre is killed by Sheriff Pat Garrett and his posse on December 23, 1880, after being mistaken for Billy the Kid. Richard M. Brewer is killed by "Buckshot" Roberts on April 4, 1878. Roberts is suffering from the stomach wound inflicted by Bowdre that will lead to his death when he kills Brewer.

61. Born 1843. McSween arrives in Lincoln March 3, 1875, and sets up a law practice. He works initially for Murphy, but becomes an enemy and joins with Tunstall to lead the anti-Murphy-Dolan faction in the Lincoln County War. He is killed at the end of the 5-day shoot-out in Lincoln, on July 19, 1878.

62. *Mesilla Valley Independent,* September 29, 1877.

63. Located on the east side of the Organ Mountains, known today as the Cox Ranch.

64. Frederick Nolan, *The Lincoln County War* (Revised Edition, 2009), pp 158-159.

65. Space limitations prevent providing more details on these men. Billy is indicted for the killing of "Buckshot" Roberts and Sheriff Frank Brady on April 18, 1878. On November 13, 1878, the Territorial Governor issues a blanket pardon for everyone involved in the Lincoln County War, except those who had been indicted already. Billy and several of his companions are the only participants who have been indicted. And in the end, Billy is the only person ever sentenced for any of the Lincoln County War deaths. He is tried in Mesilla, in the courthouse opposite the Corn Exchange Hotel, during the April, 1881, term of the Third Judicial District Court. See note 66, Chapter 2.

66. *"The Boyhood of Billy the Kid,"* Robert N. Mullin, Southwestern Studies Monograph No. 17, 1967.

67. *"Apprenticeship of an Outlaw, 'Billy the Kid' in Arizona,"* Jerry Weddle, The Journal of Arizona History, Vol. 31, No. 3, Autumn, 1990, p 236.

68. This comparison can't be made with the black and white images in this book.

69. *San Diego Union,* August 3, 1876.

70. The last entry in the Corn Exchange Hotel Register is November 26, 1878.

71. *Mesilla News,* February 1, 1879.

72. *Mesilla News,* April 26, 1879.

73. Lease: Agustina Davis to W. R. Simpson, term of lease: May 1, 1879 to May 1, 1880, renewable until 1884.

74. *Mesilla News,* May 17, 1879.

75. *Mesilla News,* June 14, 1879.

76. *Thirty-Four,* August 29, 1879.

77. *Watertown Daily Times,* Sept 2, 1884.

78. *Thirty Four,* October 20, 1880.

79. *Rio Grande Republican,* March 4, 1882.

80. Gordon Owen, *Las Cruces New Mexico 1849-1999* (1999), pp 48-52.

81. *Rio Grande Republican,* June 24, 1882.

82. Agustina Davis probate file, Doña Ana Courthouse.

83. Agustina Davis probate file, Doña Ana Courthouse.

84. Born July 16, 1846, into a wealthy family at St. Germain Lembron, France. Father Grange is assigned to St. Genevieve's (Las Cruces) in 1882. It is unknown if this is his first appointment as parish priest. In 1886, he transfers to San Albino, where he is elevated to Monsignor. The cost of the new San Albino Church is $15,000, of which Father Grange contributes more than $8,500. He dies January 6, 1936, and is buried behind San Albino's.

85. Agustina Davis probate file, Doña Ana Courthouse.

Billy the Kid Museum

The Mesilla Billy the Kid Museum, once nationally famous, is dispersed now into the hands of anonymous collectors. George Weart Griggs spent decades acquiring the museum's treasures -- *"a million dollar collection"* -- in Mexico and the United States.

George Weart Griggs

Griggs is born in Mesilla on May 2, 1866, making him one the first generation of Mesilleros.[1] When he is 11 years old, his father James Edgar Griggs[2] dies in a freak carriage accident.[3] By 1880, when the census is taken, both George, age 14, and his older sister, age 16, are in boarding school in California.[4][5] In 1887, aged 21, he is attending St. Michael's College in Santa Fe.[6]

Following graduation at St. Michael's, seeking adventure and additional education, he travels to Mexico, where he obtains an advanced degree.[7]

It is unclear when he graduates in Mexico and returns to the United States, but by August, 1894, he owns the Star Stables in El Paso. Besides renting and repairing livery, buying and selling horses, he performs undertaking and embalming.[8] He sells the business a year later.[9]

After several years working in Mesilla[10], Griggs obtains a job in Janos, Mexico.[11] His mother[12] was born in Janos and her extended family live there, which likely explains how he obtains this work. Twelve months later he takes a position as postmaster of Casas Grandes, Mexico.[13] Casas Grandes is the location of the *"largest prehistoric pueblo known in the U. S. Southwest and northern Mexico."* The site consists of over 2000 rooms and was occupied from about 1140 to 1430 A. D.[14] If this is not where Griggs obtains his interest in history and artifacts, it likely stimulates it.

Griggs' next employment opportunity is unexpected -- and one that gets him lots of press in California:

"A Surprise Awaited the Postmaster of Nueva Casas Grandes -- Geronimo Ascarate's Good Fortune"

"George Griggs, postmaster of Nueva Casas Grandes, who went through recently on his way to Lower California to accompany the household effects of Geronimo Ascarate, when he got to his destination found awaiting him an appointment as secretary for Ascarate." [15]

Geronimo R. Ascarate[16] is the new Lieutenant Governor of the Mexican Territory of Lower (Baja) California, an appointment he gets from Mexican President Porfirio Diaz on August 15, 1900.[17] As the *San Diego Weekly Union* notes in a front-page story, Ascarate's first official decision is to hire *"his nephew Jorge Azcarate Griggs as his secretary."* [18]

"Jorge" Griggs tells the press that *"the efforts of the new [Lt.] governor [will be] to make it pleasant for Americans to do business"* in Tijuana [Mexico].[19] On September 20, 1900, in celebration of the 90th year of Mexican Independence, Griggs reads the Mexican Declaration of Independence to a jubilant crowd in Tijuana. This is followed by the Mexican National Anthem, a 21-cannon salute, and a parade.[20]

Eleven months later, Griggs takes a job *"as assistant manager to an English mining syndicate in Guanacevi, Chihuahua, Mexico."* [21] His decision to quit as Azcarate's secretary is possibly motivated by legal trouble that Ascarate's boss, Governor Agustín Sanginés gets into, which leads eventually to Sanginés being sent to prison.[22]

In later years, Griggs claimed to have been the *"acting governor"* of Lower California, a claim repeated in his obituary.[23] A list of those governors shows he is never governor, nor is it likely an American would be appointed to that position, but he could have been the effective governor while Governor Sanginés struggled with his legal problems.[24].

Shortly after arriving in Chihuahua, Griggs is appointed director of the Chihuahua Permanent Mineral Display, a Chihuahuan state agency created to promote mining in the state of Chihuahua. Griggs holds this position, which is apparently quite lucrative, for the next 10 years:

> *"George Griggs Azcarate, a wealthy resident of Chihuahua, is visiting Juarez and El Paso on a vacation, which will be largely spent in California. Mr. Azcarate is in charge of the mining exposition at the state capital, and known by mining men throughout northern Mexico and the southwest."* [25]

The experiences of these years lead to Griggs' first two books: **Primer Diccionario de la Lengua Tarahumara,** a dictionary of the language of the Tarahumara Indians of Chihuahua,[26] and **Mines of Chihuahua, 1911: History, Geology, Statistics, Mining Companies.**[27] Both books sell well and go into multiple editions. His dictionary of Tarahumara, researched by living for several months among the Tarahumara in an isolated, mountainous village, is the first published for that language.[28]

In 1911, the Mexican Revolution erupts, forcing Griggs to flee Mexico. He walks from Monterey, Mexico, to Eagle Pass, Texas.[29]

Back in the United States, Griggs moves to El Paso, where his mother is now living. [30] Perhaps trying to earn a living as a writer, he publishes two pieces in the El Paso press. The first is a translation from the French of an article by Count Leo Tolstoi praising Porfirio Diaz. Diaz was forced from power and into exile in France by the Mexican Revolution. Tolstoi's position is that Diaz had made *"order out of chaos"* in Mexico, and that Diaz was Mexico's best hope for democracy.[31]

Griggs' second piece is a Christmas story entitled *"Conchita's Christmas Tree."* [32]

On August 13, 1913, Griggs takes a job as Spanish teacher *"in the grades"* at Bailey School[33] at $100 per month.[34]

Four months later Griggs is forced to resign because an intended good deed is taken instead as an insult:

> *"'I resigned because I was asked to,' read the letter of George Griggs.... Mr. Griggs stated that during his experience as a Spanish teacher... he had trouble only with Miss Anna Ray Moss, a teacher at the Bailey school, and one of the students, who pulled his coat tails. Miss Moss, he said, refused to shake hands with him. One day... when he and Miss Moss got on a street car together he paid both fares. Miss Moss... told the conductor to give him back her fare as she would not have 'any man paying her fare.'"* [35]

With the loss of this teaching job, it is unclear how he earns a living, but during the next two years he enhances his reputation for scholarship. In a small piece in the El Paso Herald, he explains the origin of the term *"Xmas."* [36] Then in October, 1916, at the request of the *El Paso Herald* editor, he writes a multiple-page article on the history of the Mesilla Valley and El Paso del Norte. The article quotes numerous early Spanish and Mexican documents that Griggs has collected, as well as documents from the Mexican-American and Civil War periods. In discussing the origins of the first Native Americans in New Mexico, he mentions Casas Grandes and the many valuable relics that have been found there.[37]

In November, 1917, Griggs gets an unusual job – rationalizing the streets of Las Cruces and assigning numbers to the city's houses.[38] Prior to this, none of the houses in Las Cruces had house numbers. Mail is delivered based on the person it is addressed to – part of the job of the postmaster is to know where to find an addressee.

He starts by specifying the geographical center of the town: *"the point where Main Street is intersected by Griggs street."* [39] Based on that, Griggs then assigns *"south"* to all streets south of Griggs street and *"north"* to all streets north of Griggs street. All streets west of Main street are assigned *"west"* and all streets east of Main street are assigned *"east."* Thus, this creates, for example, a South Water street and a North Water street. An example of the east-west axis is West Amador and East Amador. The center point also determines North and South Main streets and West and East Griggs streets.

With the streets assigned rational names, Griggs then assigns numbers to the houses:

> *"All even numbers are on the north of streets running east and west. Of the streets running north and south, the even numbers are on the east, the odd on the west. 100 to a block."* [40]

As the world's greatest expert on Las Cruces addresses, Griggs takes the next natural step. He takes the civil service examination for postal clerk[41] and is hired by the Las Cruces post office.[42]

While working as postal clerk, he issues a new version of his ***Mines of Chihuahua, 1911: History, Geology, Statistics, Mining Companies.***[43] He also publishes a series of articles on the history of Mesilla in the *Las Cruces Citizen.*[44]

Museum

On November 23, 1923, Griggs' mother dies. She still owns property in Mesilla, which her three living children inherit. This includes the original Griggs homestead built by James Edgar Griggs in 1874.[45] The author believes that this also includes a house in Mesilla on the corner of Calle de Parian and Calle de San Albino, into which Griggs moves, but no deed record has been found.[46]

By 1925, Griggs has established his Billy the Kid museum at the Calle de Parian and Calle de San Albino location. Like all private museums, it's not theme-based, in spite of its name. Griggs simply puts on display the materials he has collected during his lifetime. These include Billy the Kid documents and artifacts; original Spanish and Mexican documents; Civil War documents; a *"breeches"* Bible; old maps and pictures; paintings; religious relics; pictures and possessions of Emperor Maximilian and Empress Carlotta[47]; imported porcelain and china vases; silver vases; antique furniture; over 50 rifles and pistols, including some very early models; military swords; cannon balls, flags, old coins and currency, including Confederate *"rag"* currency once used in Mesilla; Native American artifacts, axes, and stone tools; arrow heads; and prehistoric bones and fossils.[48]

Among the items in his Billy the Kid collection is a rifle once owned by Billy, the chair in which he had his last haircut before his trial, and one of the original warrants issued for Billy's arrest for killing Sheriff Brady.

Griggs charges 25 cents to visit the museum.[49]

In October of 1925, the Spanish newspaper *La Prensa* publishes a long article based on Griggs' collection of *"volumes and parchments written by Spanish friars."* [50]

On February 2, 1926, Griggs purchases the La Posta property from Father Grange for $500.[51] It is unclear what his plans for the building are; apparently it is rented as housing.

In 1930, Griggs publishes **History of Mesilla Valley or the Gadsden Purchase, Known in Mexico as the Treaty of Mesilla.**[52] The book is well-received and is still a valuable resource for historians.

In late 1932, Griggs announces plans to take his Billy the Kid Museum exhibits to the Chicago World Fair, a plan that evidently falls through.[53]

A few years later, Griggs' attempt to add to his collection gets him into legal trouble:

> *"The mystery of the disappearance of an oil mural of the Virgin of Our Lady of Guadalupe from the Catholic Church at Guadalupe... was cleared up today...."*
>
> *"Federal Judge Miguel Mendoza Lopez of Juarez said the mural was taken from the church sacristy by George Griggs of Mesilla after he asked the church caretaker if he could have the old painting and an old Missal which were gathering dust in the room...."*

"A group of Guadalupe Indians, offended because they believed the painting of their patron saint had been sold [by the caretaker] ... threatened violence...."

"Mr. Griggs said he obtained the painting on his promise to replace it with a new one from Cincinnati, Ohio."

"'I was afraid that in Guadalupe it might be destroyed by some person opposed to the church,' he said. 'I wanted to preserve it in my museum because of its historical value....'"

"He added that he returned it through the Mexican section of the International Boundary Commission...." [54]

By the mid-to-late 1930s, Griggs is barely making a living. He is in his late 60s and not feeling well. He doesn't have the money or the will to repair his house/museum which, when it rains, leaks water on his collection:

"It's ruining them, but I just don't feel like doing anything about it.... I don't feel very good." [55]

His makes a number of attempts to sell his museum, but is unable to find a buyer willing to pay what he considers it to be worth. Nor does he want the collection split up and sold to different collectors.[56]

People who remember him in his last years recall him walking to get around, even between Mesilla and Las Cruces. He is fondly called *"El Conde,"* the Count, by locals because of his distinguished reputation, formal dress, *"soldierly bearing,"* and *"neatly-clipped, greying moustache and van dyke"* beard.[57]

Timeline

- May 2, 1866 -- George Weart Griggs born
- October 28, 1877 – James Edgar Griggs dies
- 1887 – Griggs attends St. Michael's College, Santa Fe
- 1894 – Griggs owns the Star Stables, El Paso
- 1897 – Griggs takes job in Janos, Mexico
- December 30, 1899 – Griggs takes job as Postmaster of Casas Grandes
- August 15, 1900 – Geronimo Ascarate appointed Lt. Governor of Lower California
- August 16, 1900 – Ascarate appoints Griggs his secretary
- August 5, 1901 – Griggs takes mining job in Guanacevi, Chihuahua
- 1902 – Griggs appointed Director of the Chihuahua Permanent Mineral Display
- 1910 – Griggs publishes ***Primer Diccionario de la Lengua Tarahumara***
- 1911 – Griggs publishes ***Mines of Chihuahua, 1911: History, Geology, Statistics, Mining Companies***
- October, 1911 – Griggs moves to El Paso
- August 13, 1913 – Griggs takes job as Spanish teacher
- December 16, 1913 – Griggs resigns as Spanish teacher
- November 10, 1917 – Griggs takes job assigning numbers to houses in Las Cruces

- March 13, 1919 – Griggs hired as postal clerk
- January 1, 1921 – Griggs publishes series on history of Mesilla
- November 23, 1923 – Eugenia Griggs dies
- 1924 – Griggs moves into house at Calle de Parian and Calle de San Albino, Mesilla
- 1925 – Griggs establishes the Billy the Kid Museum
- February 2, 1926 – Griggs buys the La Posta property from Father Grange
- 1930 – Griggs publishes *History of Mesilla Valley or the Gadsden Purchase, Known in Mexico as the Treaty of Mesilla*
- November 13, 1935 – Greggs gets in trouble after taking painting from Guadalupe church

Photos

George Weart Griggs during his time as director of the Chihuahua Permanent Mineral Display, Chihuahua, Mexico. Courtesy Frank H. Parrish.

Billy the Kid Museum established by Griggs in his house at Calle de Parian and Calle de San Albino. Circa 1926. Courtesy Archives and Special Collections, New Mexico State University.

Griggs displaying a Winchester rifle owned by Billy the Kid. Griggs had an affidavit that the rifle was taken from Billy signed by the judge who confiscated. It is unknown who the judge was. Circa 1928. Courtesy Frank H. Parrish.

Griggs standing in front of the Corn Exchange (La Posta) building. He posted the sign on the building shortly after buying it. The sign reads *"CORN EX-CHANGE HOTEL, EST 1859, George Griggs, Prop."* Note that Griggs has got the founding date wrong. Courtesy Palace of Governors Collection.

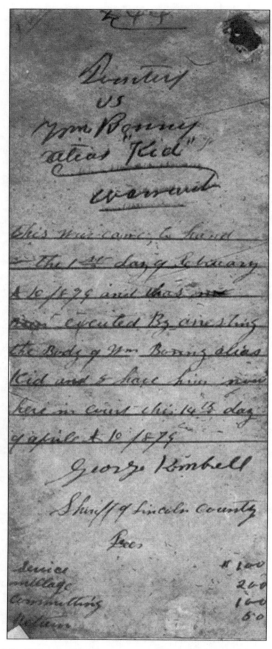

Arrest warrant for Billy the Kid that was in Griggs' Billy the Kid Museum collection. Courtesy Frank H. Parrish.

Footnotes

1. *Las Cruces Sun-News,* November 2, 1939. A Mesillero is a native of Mesilla.

2. Born August 2, 1836. By 1859, James E. Griggs is in New Mexico working as a clerk at Ft. Fillmore. In 1863 he enters into partnership with Joseph Reynolds, who had been a clerk at Ft. Fillmore also, and opens a store in Mesilla. They marry daughters of Cristobal Ascarate. James Griggs marries Eugenia Ascarate and Reynolds marries Guadalupe Ascarate.

3. *Santa Fe New Mexican,* October 30, 1877. The carriage overturns and James Griggs is struck by one of its wheels. His daughter Kate is in the carriage at the time of the accident.

4. U. S. Census, Mesilla, New Mexico, 1880.

5. *Las Cruces Sun-News,* November 2, 1939.

6. *Santa Fe Weekly Express,* July 2, 1887.

7. *"The Count of Old Mesilla,"* Desert Magazine, January, Vol. 3, No. 3, 1940.

8. *Rio Grande Republican,* April 28, 1894.

9. *Rio Grande Republican,* September 6, 1895.

10. *Dona Ana County Republican,* April 22, 1897

11. *Labrador,* December 2, 1898

12. Born Eugenia Ascarate in November, 1849. She marries James Edgar Griggs on December 16, 1866.

13. *El Paso Daily Herald,* December 30, 1899; *Dona Ana County Republican,* April 21, 1900.

14. Susan Toby Evans and David L. Webster, editors, *Archaeology of Ancient Mexico and Central America: An Encyclopedia* (2001), p 97.

15. *El Paso Daily Herald,* August 4, 1900.

16. The author has not established the exact relationship between Geronimo and George. There is a Geronimo Ascarate that is the son of the brother of Griggs' great grandfather, but this reference is probably to a younger, more closely related Geronimo.

17. *Evening Tribune,* August 15, 1900.

18. *San Diego Weekly Union,* August 16, 1900.

19. *San Diego Weekly Union,* August 16, 1900.

20. *San Diego Weekly Union,* September 20, 1900.

21. *San Diego Union,* August 5, 1901.

22. *Los Angeles Herald,* July 2, 1902.

23. *Las Cruces Sun-News,* November 2, 1939.

24. Web site: en.wikipedia.org/wiki/Governor_of_Baja_California

25. *El Paso Daily Herald,* July 14, 1910.

26. Talleres Tipograficos de la Escuela de Artes y Oficios a Cargo de M. A. Gomez, Chihuahua, Mexico, 1910.

27. Imp. El Norte, Chihuahua, Mexico, 1911.

28. *Las Cruces Sun-News,* November 2, 1939.

29. *Las Cruces Sun-News,* November 2, 1939.

30. U. S. Census, Precinct 1, El Paso, Texas, 1900.

31. *El Paso Herald,* September 12, 1912.

32. *El Paso Herald,* December 24, 1912.

33. Founded in 1889 as Mesa School. Renamed after first principal Bessie Bailey in 1912. El Paso, 1850-1950, James R. Murphy, p 54.

34. *El Paso Herald,* September 13, 1913.

35. *El Paso Herald,* December 16, 1913.

36. *El Paso Herald,* December 8, 1915. Griggs writes that "X" stands for the Greek letter "Ch," an abbreviation for "Christos," and Mas is short for Mass.

37. *El Paso Herald,* October 7, 1916.

38. *El Paso Herald,* November 10, 1917.

39. Griggs street is named after Griggs' father – not by Griggs, but many years earlier.

40. *El Paso Herald,* November 10, 1917.

41. *El Paso Herald,* November 22, 1918.

42. *El Paso Herald,* March 13, 1919.

43. *El Paso Herald,* March 13, 1919.

44. *El Paso Herald,* January 1, 1921.

45. *Mesilla News,* May 9, 1874.

46. The lot today is a parking lot for La Posta.

47. Placed in power as Emperor of Mexico on April 10, 1864, by Napoleon III of France and aristocratic monarchists in Mexico. Opposed by revolting forces led by Benito Juarez, he was captured and executed on June 19, 1867. His last request is that he *"not be shot in the face."*

48. George Griggs probate file, Doña Ana Courthouse; *"The Count of Old Mesilla,"* Desert Magazine.

49. "The Count of Old Mesilla," Desert Magazine, January, Vol. 3, No. 3, 1940.

50. *La Prensa,* October 30, 1925.

51. Rev. Juan Grange to George Griggs, Feb 2, 1926, Book 73, p 19.

52. Bronson Print Company, 1930.

53. *El Paso Herald-Post,* December 13, 1932.

54. *El Paso Herald-Post,* November 13, 1935.

55. *El Paso Herald-Post,* November 6, 1939.

56. *El Paso Herald-Post,* November 16, 1935; *El Paso Herald-Post,* January 11, 1936.

57. Notes by Dan Aranda; *"The Count of Old Mesilla,"* Desert Magazine.

Chapter 5 | La Posta Restaurant

Katherine Griggs Camunez

In mid-1939, Katherine *"Katy"* Griggs Camunez approaches George Griggs with a plan to open a restaurant in Mesilla, and asks about renting the Corn Exchange property. Camunez is Griggs' niece, the daughter of his brother Gustave Griggs. Griggs agrees.

The old building is *"in run-down condition -- some of its windows and doors boarded up, its wall crumbling, part of the rooms... outlined only by tumble-down adobes."* Katy, as her patrons affectionately call her, has *"only $1.25 in 'working capital'"* to turn the building into a restaurant.[1]

On September 16, 1939, she opens *"La Posta"* in one room in the building, equipped with *"three tables and 12 chairs."* [2] The name comes from the widely-held belief at the time that the building had once been the stage stop for the Butterfield Overland Mail Line.

The restaurant is an immediate success, running *"out of food, almost every night."* Katy's mother does the cooking initially, based on family recipes. *"Soon an adjoining room [is] refinished and opened... [and] more tables and chairs [are] moved in."* [3]

With all signs indicating success, Katy asks to purchase the building. Griggs agrees and sells it to her on October 21, 1939, for one dollar.[4] When he signs the deed, which he does with a mark, Griggs is in bed and acutely ill.[5]

On November 2, 1939, Griggs dies.[6] His home and museum are inherited by his brothers and sisters. The worry of interested, outside parties is that the museum will be split up. An attempt is made *Las Cruces Sun-News* columnist Wallace Perry to convince a public-spirited donor or officials in Las Cruces or Mesilla to buy the museum:

> *"For the sake of the memory of the man himself – as well as for the sake of his home community – it seems to me that the Griggs collection should be converted, intact, into the nucleus of a museum for the community in which he was born, and in which he passed the last years of his life."* [7]

That effort fails.

In March, 1940, Gustave Griggs exhibits the museum in his home, which probably is not the most satisfactory arrangement.[8] A couple of months later the museum is put on display in La Posta, where it is quite successful, attracting 522 visitors in just the first month.[9] For the next three years, the museum continues to draw visitors, including various notables, which are duly reported in the *Las Cruces Sun-News*. For example, the *"Chewing Gum King"* William Wrigley, Jr. visits in March, 1941.[10]

The Japanese attack on Pearl Harbor on December 7, 1941, forces to the United States into World War II. One of the lesser-known consequences of the war is that tourism in the United States drops precipitously. With the drafting of millions, the enormous diversion of labor to the war effort, and the rationing of food, gas, tires, and other goods, tourism is a luxury that few have the time, money, or desire to pursue.

To make the museum more accessible and increase visitors, it is moved from La Posta to Las Cruces in March, 1944.[11] There it is displayed at the Casa de Las Cruces, which is also a gift shop.[12] The museum remains in Las Cruces for two years, after which it returns to La Posta.[13]

The Billy The Kid Museum continues to be part of La Posta until the mid-to-late 50s,[14] when it is moved to Griggs' Restaurant in El Paso. There, sometime in the 70s, the collection is broken up and many of the artifacts sold to private collectors.

La Posta Today

The restaurant started in such a humble fashion in 1939 by Katy Griggs Camunez in the building owned by Nestor Varela, Sam and Roy Bean, Marshal Abraham Cutler, Leopoldo Carrillo, John Lemon, Lola Bennett, John Davis, Agustina Davis, Father Juan Grange, and George Griggs is now famous world-wide. From the early 50s, restaurant guides and national publications such as *Life Magazine* and *The Saturday Evening Post* listed it as *"the place"* to visit in southern New Mexico. Virtually all visitors to the area, from then until now, ensure that they eat at La Posta at least once.

When you consider the 70-plus years that the restaurant has been in business, it is hard to doubt that it has drawn more people to Mesilla than all other attractions and businesses in the town combined.

Buen provecho! Buen apetito! Que aproveche!

Timeline

- September 16, 1939 – Katy Camunez opens La Posta
- October 21, 1939 – Griggs sells Corn Exchange lot to Katy Camunez
- November 2, 1939 – George Griggs dies
- March, 1944 – Billy The Kid Museum moves to Las Cruces
- October, 1946 – Museum moves to La Posta
- Late 50s – Museum moves to Griggs Restaurant in El Paso
- Mid-70s – Collection dispersed

Photos

Griggs with Katherine Griggs Camunez and daughter in front of the Griggs'
homestead, Mesilla. 1939. Courtesy Archives and Special Collections, New
Mexico State University.

Griggs outside of La Posta. 1939. Courtesy Frank H. Parrish.

Griggs speaking with unidentified person in courtyard of La Posta. 1939. Courtesy Archives and Special Collections, New Mexico State University.

La Posta shortly after opening. 1939-40. Courtesy of Palace of Governors Collection.

La Posta, late 1940s or early 1950s.

Billy the Kid Museum, La Posta, early 1950s.

Billy the Kid Museum, La Posta, early 1950s.

La Posta, early 1950s. Courtesy of the Palace of Governors Collection.

La Posta, 1960s.

Footnotes

1. *Las Cruces Sun-News,* July 3, 1941.

2. *Las Cruces Sun-News,* July 3, 1941.

3. *Las Cruces Sun-News,* July 3, 1941.

4. George Griggs to Katherine Griggs Camunez, Oct 21, 1939.

5. *Las Cruces Sun-News,* October 22, 1939.

6. *Las Cruces Sun-News,* November 2, 1939.

7. *Las Cruces, Sun-News,* November 5, 1939.

8. *Las Cruces Sun-News,* March 11, 1940.

9. *Las Cruces Sun-News,* May 28, 1940.

10. *Las Cruces Sun-News,* March 3, 1941.

11. *Las Cruces Sun-News,* March 15, 1944.

12. *Las Cruces Sun-News,* July 3, 1944.

13. *Las Cruces Sun-News,* October 8, 1946; *Las Cruces Sun-News,* March 1, 1971.

14. *Las Cruces Sun-News,* March 1, 1953.

Index

Doc45 Publications:

- Torpedo Squadron Four: A Cockpit View of World War II
- Torpedo Squadron Four - Photo Supplement
- A Winding Road To The Land Of Enchantment
- The Academic Ecosystem